Country Matters

Contents

Contents

Acknowledgements

The author and publishers would like to thank the following for permission to reproduce the photographs and cartoons in this book: the folios refer to the chapter in which they appear.

Derek Johnson: 1b, 21, 40
Robin Williams: 3, 14, 20b, 22, 24, 26, 34, 38, 43, 47, 63, 67
Stanley Porter: 5, 17, 45
The Guide Dogs for the Blind Association: 7
Dave Parfitt: 9, 11, 41, 57, 62, 66
R. J. C. Blewitt: 10
Michael Clark: 13, 18, 50, 54, 55
R. P. Lawrence: 15, 31, 58
Bill Wilkinson: 20a, 28, 48, 53
Birmingham Evening Mail: 29, 35, 39, 51, 64, 68
H. K. Bowen Photographs: 1c, 37
Western Morning News: 59
George Ingar: 60

Foreword

I am lucky enough to earn my living working with pleasant country-men in lovely country places. To add to my good fortune, I live in a cottage a mile from the nearest main road with mixed woodland that I manage as a wildlife reserve. So it is my privilege to share my good fortune with other country lovers, often based in towns, by writing and broadcasting about my life and surroundings.

It is my belief that too many people are obsessed with the cult of rarity. Birdwatchers will travel hundreds of miles to tick-off some foreign rarity on their check-list of birds it is, in theory, possible to see in these islands. The fact that it would never have arrived if it had not been blown off-course by a freak storm means nothing to them. All that matters is that it is a fresh name on their little lists. No wonder such folk are nicknamed Twitchers!

I get as much pleasure and interest from robins and swallows that come willingly to my garden as from any exotic freak. And, so I find, do the majority of my readers. My post bag is fuller after an article about a mistle thrush that chivvies lesser birds from the bird table than when I write about rare migrants that few will ever have the chance to see.

Having learned my trade more from poachers and gamekeepers than from academic school gaffers, I see the countryside 'warts and all'. Sentimentalists throw up their hands when men chase foxes with hounds but never bat an eye when the same men go ratting with terriers.

I believe that there is room in the countryside for a very wide variety of interests and, provided that they do not imperil an endangered species, I consider it is no business of mine how others amuse themselves.

But I did what I could to encourage a law to ban otter hunting, because otters really are an endangered species and hunting could well have been the last straw. However, since they are so shy that disturbance involving no physical injury will prevent them breeding, I am as keen to prevent anglers and mink hunters and ramblers disturbing them as I am to guard them from otter hounds.

Unfortunately, so far as the countryside goes, the law is often as big an ass as legend paints it.

In 1973, an act was passed to protect badgers, for centuries our most persecuted of wild creatures. Now, the Ministry of Agriculture is exterminating them on a scale never dreamed of by traditional badger diggers and baiters. Their 'crime' of transmitting bovine TB has never been proved, although they are doubtless fellow victims. But, in any case, the ministry cure(!) is not working and never can work because their action actually forces badgers to move to fresh territory and, after squandering £600,000 and the lives of more than 10,000 badgers, TB in cattle is spreading faster than before.

The Wildlife and Countryside Bill, passed last year, tries to be all things to all men and has achieved very little. So, from time to time, I have a knock at that!

This book is a selection, made by my publisher, from my weekly column in the *Birmingham Evening Mail*. I have been writing for the paper regularly since 1964 and I try to cover as wide a canvas of natural history and country life as I can, choosing subjects that are of interest to me, in the hope that my readers will share my pleasure – or occasionally anger!

So my thanks are due to the Editor of the *Evening Mail* for allowing me to air my views, which I trust will help to leave the countryside better than I found it, both in his paper and reprinted here in this book.

PHIL DRABBLE
Summer 1982

The author with Belle and Tick

1. Love Me, Love My Dog

Mick, my first dog, was my constant companion from when I was eight until he died when I was nearly twenty. We had marvellous times together, ratting and rabbiting or simply 'mooching' about in quiet places. As an only child, I was shy and diffident about striking up new acquaintances, but Mick took care of that. He was an extrovert with the supreme belief that all real 'dogmen', which included everyone with a common love of dogs, was bound to like his master. His introductions knew no bounds of class or creed. Through Mick I met the local squire – and many of the poachers who shared his game. I became friends with prosperous farmers, with Hairy Kelly, the local rat-catcher and with Constable 'Jago' Smith, who owned a famous whippet and was addicted to ferreting, as Mick and I were.

Since those days I have had a constant succession of good, working dogs in whose company I have rubbed shoulders with the most delightful people, all of whom share a common love of dogs. It occurred to me that strangers might also like to meet my friends and the dogs which are our common bond, so I put up the idea of a series of programmes about them for television. As a result, I never enjoyed myself so much – or worked so hard! We called the series 'It's a Dog's Life' and I spent most of the summer of 1979 recording just what went on behind the scenes with five very different breeds of working dogs.

The first programme was about the Quorn foxhounds, filmed at their Leicestershire kennels, where I was privileged to see what went on out of the hunting season. The problems of keeping more than fifty couples of hounds healthy under conditions that would have been rated heavy stocking by farmers, were formidable. Kennel hygiene has to be clinical and the way Michael Farrin the huntsman memorised more than a hundred names – and never failed to fit them to the right hound – left me speechless. I went out on dewy summer dawns to watch hounds at exercise, made new friends, from professional huntsmen to local farmers, and, as always when I meet new dogmen, I learned a lot I didn't know before.

'Keep running, and don't fall over!' Phil at the Police
Dog Training School at Stafford.

Love Me, Love My Dog

To give some idea of the variety of people in the series, one day I lunched with five masters of fox hounds, and the next I had an equally happy evening with the whippet men at a miners' club in Cannock! Doing this programme on running dogs was like re-living my childhood because Alf Sargeant, a barber who lived opposite our house in Bloxwich, was a famous whippet-racer when I was a child. He used to train his dogs on some waste ground outside my bedroom window and, on summer evenings when I was supposed to be fast asleep, I used to creep out of bed to spy on the tricks of his trade. It bred a burning ambition to have a whippet of my own, but my old man, who was a highly respectable doctor, said nobody would keep a poacher's dog in his house . . . so I had to wait until I was married!

Filming whippets for television at Cannock was enormous fun. I met many old friends and made new ones, some of whom had been patients in the days when whippets were forbidden ground to me. We saw the modern dogs at home and on holiday, in the smoky bar and at full stretch on the track, and we contrasted this participant sport with the spectator sport of greyhound racing on one of the Birmingham dog tracks.

I spent one of the wettest days of my life at a retriever field trial, and one of the most inspiring weeks watching blind owners being introduced to their guide dogs before setting out to explore new worlds together.*

There were exciting times too. I own a much-loved Alsatian which the show-dog folk insist on calling a German Shepherd, because Alsatians have a reputation for being fierce. I wanted to show what Alsatians are really like when properly trained as police dogs, since I am a firm believer that there are no bad dogs – only bad owners. The police at the dog-training school at Stafford were delighted to help, so we saw a new intake of handlers introduced to their dogs and we called several times during the thirteen-week course to see how men and dogs were getting on. The early part of the training really applied to any dog and I learned a lot about how to train my own dog to come when she is called, sit where she is told, walk quietly at heel and the other basic exercises that all civilised household pets should know.

*see also No. 7

The excitement for me came when the dogs were advanced enough to learn to help detain criminals. They start by getting them to chase a rag for fun, and then they wrap the rag round a protective leather sleeve so that when they grab it, they grab the 'criminal's' arm, which it envelopes. It looked simple enough, so, liking to speak from experience, I asked the instructor if I could have a go. He looked at me as if I'd gone daft and said that I certainly could – but he would take no responsibility if things went wrong. So I put on the sleeve and asked him if he had any tips.

'Keep your eye on the dog,' he said, 'so that you can feed the padded part into his mouth. Keep running and, for goodness' sake, don't fall over. You can't control where he bites you if you fall over.'

Very funny, in retrospect. But not such a joke when you see a hairy great Alsatian (shepherd dogs, my foot!) coming for you with malice aforethought! However, I got on all right, and did enjoy making the programme.

NOTE: Having been involved with dogs all my life, and found that so many nice people like nice, well-trained dogs, I am sharing my experiences of pleasant dogs I have known by writing my next book about them.

2. Polecat Pedigrees

I don't believe in polecats, or at least I didn't until a short while ago. My reason for being sceptical about the existence of what the books assert is a native British mammal is because I believe ferrets are domesticated polecats and in any area where polecats could survive there are certain to be lots of rabbits for them to feed on. Where there are lots of rabbits, the local countrymen will have been catching them with ferrets for generations.

Some of them will have lost ferrets, which will have returned to the habits of their wild ancestors and interbred with any genuinely wild polecats that were there before them. So my belief has always been that the animals which are often reported as road casualties are probably ferrets gone wild or polecats with a lot of ferret blood. Research biologists say this is rubbish. They say ferrets are not domesticated polecats but a slightly different species which they can distinguish but ignorant amateurs cannot.

I take their point! But recently, when I was at the Game Fair, I called at the pugs and drummers stand. Pugs, in the jargon of sporting gents, are ferrets, which are certainly aggressive enough to qualify as pugilists. Drummers are the rabbits, which thump the ground with their hind feet, as a sort of tom-tom warning to other rabbits that danger is about. The pugs and drummers stand displays all sorts of rabbitting equipment, from spades to sophisticated electronic devices designed to locate errant ferrets which stay underground to eat the rabbit instead of driving it out to the waiting sportsmen.

There is also a ferret mart, where these delightful animals can be bought and sold. Waiting in a hutch for a buyer, there was an exceptionally dark-coloured young jill ferret with which I fell in love on sight. Common ferrets are yellowy-white with pink eyes. I believe their ancestors were albino polecats, which have been selectively bred down the centuries until they are tame and domesticated. The other common variety is the fitchet ferret, which is a browny colour with lighter markings on the head. Some folk refer to these as polecat ferrets.

15

The creature that caught my eye in the ferret mart was like a fitchet ferret, but much darker and more definitely marked. It's mother was apparently an ordinary fitchet ferret, which I saw, and its father was a wild-caught polecat which had been introduced to the ferret at the mating season. I suppose beauty is in the eye of the beholder, but I have rarely seen a creature I thought more lovely, so I parted with her purchase price and came away with her in my poacher's pocket.

At first she behaved like an ordinary ferret. She let me pick her up and handle her without any complaints. Having had ferrets all my life, I know they are not the savage beasts ignorant folk believe. They only bite in fear and, provided they are handled a great deal while they are too young to do any damage, they lose their fear and allow themselves to be picked up as freely as a domestic cat. I got my new arrival to about this stage when I showed her to a friend.

The moment she sensed a stranger, her tail fluffed out and she spat defiance with the fury of a cat facing a strange dog. Not only did she display her apprehension with fearsome hisses, but she let off a powerful pong that was enough to knock you down. 'Stink like a polecat' is no idle phrase. Ferrets, stoats, weasels, otters and polecats all have a gland under their tails which contains musk. This is used to mark territory, and, in small doses, is pleasant enough to be put in ladies' perfume. But when a cloud of it is set free, there is no doubt the animal wishes to be left alone!

As she grew, my young ferret – or crossbred polecat? – showed more and more wild characteristics. She is as agile as a stoat and can enter her nest box with a flying leap that takes her through the small hole at full toss, without touching the sides. She loves raw pigeon or rabbit but will not touch butcher's meat or bread and milk. I once gave her a raw egg and watched what happened. The curvature of the shell was too great for her to pinch between her teeth and it was too hard and smooth to puncture. So she shoved it with her head as a dog will play circus football with a rubber ball. She 'dribbled' it round and round her pen until, at last, it cracked so hard into the wall the shell shattered. I never saw a ferret that was so inventive.

As she grew, her games became rougher and now her bites occasionally draw blood. The next week or so will be crucial. Either she will revert to the wild, and it will be impossible to handle her without a thick glove – or she will accept me as an equal and tolerate my ways. I still don't know if she is an ordinary ferret or whether her sire was wild with the blood of wild polecats or merely escaped ferrets. What I do know is that it will be a challenge to gentle her, over the next few weeks, so I can continue to appreciate her charms without getting too many sore thumbs!

3.   Katie's Kestrel

Kate sounds a honey and what's more she is not a bad artist either. Like so many small girls of nine she began her letter, 'Dear Mr Drabble, I hope you are well. I hope Tick is well too.'

Tick is my German short-haired pointer who steals the hearts of so many dog-lovers from old ladies to charming kids like Kate. To impress me, Kate enclosed a sample of her own artistry, a portrait of a tawny owl – now pinned, with other treasures, on my study wall. Kate is obviously pretty struck on birds of prey because her letter continues: 'We have a kestrel named Hereward. We got him from . . .' (here she gives the name of an animal dealer). 'Hereward is getting friendly now and is very good at flying and coming to the lure.'

For those not acquainted with the ancient art of falconry, the lure is a piece of fur or feather tied to a piece of string which is whirled round the head to persuade a hawk that it is its quarry so it will fly down and allow its owner to catch it. Kate explains that she got Hereward in July.

'When we are flying him, all the swallows bomb him and he gets very annoyed. We had to go to the station to collect him and he was in a big box with a handle. Sometimes he catches his own prey – mice and daddy longlegs. We have to be careful with the dog and cat when he is on his weathering perch.'

A lovely story. Until you think about it.

What a life for a wild hawk. Tied by the leg to a weathering perch, when all he wants is the freedom of the sky. Swallows spattering him with impunity. Imprisoned, he has no chance of taking evasive action if the dog and cat come by. Not Kate's fault. When I was a kid there would have been nothing that I should have liked better than a present like Hereward. Not dad's fault, either. I am sure he is convinced nothing but good comes from giving his daughter the chance to grow up with a love for wild things. But the harsh fact remains: hawks and falcons are among the wildest of wild birds which crave, above all else, their freedom.

So whose fault is it that this young bird and probably the other fledglings from the same nest has fetched up as a child's pet to be loved and spoilt – or neglected – as the whims of its young owner dictate? I accept part of the blame. I have spent the last twenty years or so writing and broadcasting about country topics and share with similar writers the responsibility of feeding the fire which has driven so many town folk to take their relaxation in quiet places. It is a short step from wanting to go out and watch wild birds to wanting to become even more closely involved by keeping one at home. The more visibly one paints word pictures of the countryside, the more people will be encouraged to put pressure on sensitive places.

But if nobody cared, what would be the chances of passing laws for the protection of birds or badgers or other endangered species? The law may be an ass in many matters but it excels where conservation is concerned. The explosion of public interest in wildlife has applied

A kestrel with the freedom of the sky

enough preasure to get laws for bird protection and the Badgers' Act passed. But MPs are slippery customers and usually leave enough loopholes to be sure constituents with opposing views are not antagonised. It is illegal for a fisherman to shoot a heron unless it is doing damage to a fishery! The rat-catchers of the Ministry of Agriculture are legally entitled to exterminate whole colonies of badgers with poison gas. What a load of rubbish!

Hawks and falcons have suddenly become valuable export items to our oil-rich masters in the Middle East, so there is considerable incentive to take young birds from the nest to sell them. This, of course, is illegal, but it is not illegal to breed wild birds in captivity and subsequently to trade in them. In order to prove they were bred in captivity, a small ring has to be slipped over their foot and on to their leg while they are still too young to fend for themselves. When they are adult it is impossible to remove the ring because the foot is then too big for it to pass over, so 'close-rung' birds are legal merchandise. What happens now is that bird traders visit nests twice instead of once. The first time, they put rings on the young bird's legs and on their return visit just before the birds are big enough to fly they are removed to cages from which they can subsequently be sold as close-rung.

So I have written to young Kate to check that her bird is close-rung. I expect it is. If not, the dealer can expect a visit from the Royal Society for the Protection of Birds and also, I hope, conviction.

NOTE: Although the Wildlife and Countryside Bill has tightened regulations, in theory, it is still possible to obtain a licence to keep a hawk, even when the keeper has unsuitable accommodation and little specialist knowledge.

The value of peregrine falcons has soared to many hundreds of pounds and a large number of falcons are poached from their eeries – un-rung – and exported illegally to the Middle East.

Only the weight of public opinion, backed up by laws with teeth, will stop this trade, and exhibitions of glamorous falcons at the Game Fair and other sporting occasions do nothing to help.

4. Frog-March To The Pool

We had a plague of frogs last week that would have delighted the heart of Moses. Moses, if you remember, visited plagues of frogs, lice, flies, locusts, darkness and death on the Egyptians in his efforts to persuade King Pharaoh that the Children of Israel were more trouble than they were worth and it would be more comfortable to let them go. The book of Exodus describes how Moses brought frogs from the river and caused them to go into Pharaoh's house and into his bedchamber – even into his bed. They covered the land of Egypt, causing Pharaoh to holler for mercy but Moses softened his heart too soon. The frogs died and they put them in heaps which made the land stink. So Pharaoh changed his mind and didn't let them go until several plagues later.

Far from annoying us, our plague of frogs was a delight. Frogs have been growing scarce in England for many years now. Mechanisation of farms has caused many little pools in the corners of fields to be filled in. Tiny tadpoles, which hatch from frog-spawn, are relished as food by fish so they have great difficulty in surviving in sizeable pools where there are many fish. Many farmers now make silage instead of hay and the overflow from silage pits can be poisonous. If that seeps into ditches or little pools, it is another nail in the poor frog's coffin. Chemical pesticides are worse.

Biology classes at schools used thousands of frogs a year for dissecting in their laboratories and, although that trade has been curtailed, the frog population has never recovered from the effects. So Moses would have been hard-put to call down a plague of frogs in England. Or so I thought.

Recently, I changed my mind. I was watching my wife weeding her flower beds when she pointed out a tiny frog about as big as a new halfpenny piece. Then another and another and another. The whole garden seemed alive with little frogs.

When I was at school, it was fashionable to collect frog-spawn in spring and keep it in an aquarium. In about three weeks it hatched into tadpoles which we fed with minute water weeds called algae and, as

21

they grew, they gradually absorbed their tails into their bodies until towards the end of summer, they had developed into perfect miniature frogs. At this stage we took them back to the pool where we had found them and let them go, believing that they stayed there all autumn and hibernated in the mud for the winter. The fact is that they migrate from the pools as surely as swallows leave our shores for Africa. They don't go as far, of course, usually not more than a few hundred yards!

The frogs in our garden have come about eighty yards from the pool where they were hatched and reared. It is quite a large pool – but there are few fish in it. The water is rather acid, because it comes over acid oak peat as it drains from the wood. It was too acid to grow many plants that would encourage insects on which all sorts of fowl could feed. So last year, I put a ton of ground limestone in the water to neutralise the acid. I knew that it would be good for plants but might be bad for any fish that were there. This didn't really matter because there would be no difficulty in introducing fresh fish when the plants began to thrive – and the plants would supply food for them.*

The fish disappeared and I am delighted to say that there is now more water-weed than I have ever seen here. But I reckon that what few fish were there took a severe bashing, leaving conditions just right for rearing tadpoles.

As the young frogs have developed, almost everything has had a bonanza. Some went up into the spinney but not many could have survived because I saw the hens simply gorging on them. The least they can do in return is to lay some double-yolked eggs! A carrion crow spent hours at the edge of the pool till I managed to get him in the sights of my rifle, but he must have had more than his share too. But you count the eggs in frog-spawn by the tens of thousands, for nature is so wasteful she allows for 99.9 per cent wastage.

The ones that came into the garden made the best choice. There is a rockery for them to creep under and hibernate for the winter. There are masses of tiny flies and aphids to feed on, and few enemies to feed on them. We spent ages admiring them. Almost wherever we looked, staccato movements of tiny frogs beginning to hop caught our eye. They were so minute that they could bathe in raindrops glistening on the

---

* *see Country Seasons*, page 52

surface of leaves and it was difficult to imagine that they would eventually develop into huge, yellow shining monsters going back to the pool of their birth to join in the cycle of reproduction.

Their skins need water to keep them moist so that they lie at the roots of plants or under stones when the weather is dry. Then, when rain does come, they all come out together and move in masses over the ground. Old books often describe how it actually rained frogs. I never believe them but I have no doubt that the explanation is the sloppy, inaccurate observation of many old writers. The truth is simply that they wait around till the air and ground are moist and then they set out on their travels.

It is a great joy to me to see creatures that are scarce elsewhere thriving on our patch. And there is no doubt in my mind that, if the ghost of Pharaoh is around, I could give Moses a few tips on precisely when to threaten him with the proverbial plague of frogs.

5.   Down To The Grass Roots

The meadow at the far end of our wood is called Daffodil Lawn because, in spring, it is famous for its display of the daintiest and most beautiful of golden wild flowers. When we came, the bulbs were still suffering from wartime efforts to wring the last ounce out of the land. The modern fashion of chemical farming may have made the grass spurt, but it did nothing for the daffs. So for the last fifteen years, we have left every flower to seed and develop new bulbs, taking care that none was picked or destroyed, and we have been equally careful they have not been contaminated by chemicals. Our reward has been a gradual recovery so that about half the field is now a glorious carpet when April comes.

Daffodil Lawn in Spring

Down To The Grass Roots

Grass, to be kept in good heart, must either be grazed or cut for hay or sileage. Left to itself, it would degenerate into a coarse mat that would look like a neglected bomb-site and strangle more delicate plants. So I have an arrangement with my neighbour who runs cattle or sheep on it from the time the daffs are over until about October. In winter, when domestic stocks are out, I throw open the gate into the wood and let the deer in for a banquet.

This year, my neighbour was shorter than usual of grass, so he asked if he could spread some bag-muck to get a bumper crop. Bag-muck, to the uninitiated, is the chemical mixture scientists dream up to increase the yields of corn and grass, so successful modern farmers can grow about twice as much corn to the acre or keep many more animals than their ancestors used to.

I was not too worried about my neighbour's cattle – but I had no intention of putting the daffs at risk. Therefore, I said he could put some bag-muck on the top half of the lawn, where there were no daffs, but none where the daffs were. Finally, we compromised by having bag-muck where it obviously could do no harm and a few tons of honest farmyard, well rotted, organic cowmuck on the rest. I calculated that a reasonable ration of God's natural fertiliser would do nothing but good. A few weeks later, before he put his cattle in, my neighbour arrived with a broad grin and an I-told-you-so expression.

'Have you been down to Daffodil Lawn lately?' he asked with an 'innocent' look on his face.

I said I had. 'So what?'

'Well, at the top end,' he said, 'there is at least twice the grass there is in the places where we only put farmyard muck. It just goes to show the manufacturers know what they are at. Enough to fatten a herd of cows, where the bag-muck is. Not enough to keep a rabbit on the rest!'

He crammed in about twenty fattening beasts, to back up his opinions, while I sat back to see if I should have to confess that old-fashioned methods might be picturesque and romantic but if it was food to feed the starving masses we wanted, the scientists had got it made. The cattle wandered all over the area first, to survey the quality of the fare on offer, and they turned up their noses at the rank, sappy mush forced up by the chemicals, rating it no higher than the pre-cooked tack served to us in far too many modern eating places. They

25

settled down, instead, to munch what they obviously regarded as the far higher quality fare, naturally grown on old pasture, and they did not even start on the intensively-fed mush at the end where the bag-muck was sown. Those cattle obviously knew exactly what they liked and were choosy enough to prefer quality to quantity.

My guess, and it is only a guess, is that beef, fed on such good old pasture might not put on weight quite so fast as intensively-fed beef, but its flavour and texture would be incomparable. I base my opinion on my own experience with other stock. The pork from pigs on free range in woodland bears little resemblance to meat normally on offer over the counter.

My job takes me all over the country and I have to eat a good deal in hotels and restaurants. I am immediately suspicious when I am offered an ostentatious menu about as big as a tabloid newspaper with a range of dishes as long as a dull sermon. It is unlikely that even quite large establishments carry such a choice of *fresh* food. The inescapable conclusion is that most of it is kept in 'boiler-bags' in the deep freeze. Flavour of real, fresh-cooked food is a thing of the past in such eating places, so taste, of a sort, is added by sousing the stuff in wine sauces or cheese or garlic or similar continental cosmetic disguises. Customers seem satisfied so long as they have been stuffed with gross enough quantities of second-rate food.

The cattle on our lawn could have taught them a lesson.

6.   The Year Of The Flies

Tetchy scientists complain that I am pachydermous. My friends accept the fact that I am simply a little thick-skinned. The two terms mean precisely the same, but boffins are notorious for trying to blind us with science, while the chaps I mix with are prone to call a spade a spade – or worse!

Whichever it is, I accept the stricture without rancour because I have long found it an advantage to be able to say what I really think without having to calculate whose corns I shall be crushing if I happen to voice an unpopular point of view. But I am far more thick-skinned than that. I have schooled myself to wander in the wood, at high summer, without experiencing an unacceptable amount of discomfort from the flies that share the atmosphere! This is a particular blessing this year.

A few years ago they dubbed it 'The Year of the Ladybird' because there were so many about that they went down the gullet of the combine harvester, with the corn, till the golden grain literally heaved with them. Some called it a 'plague' of ladybirds but, since ladybirds do so much good consuming greenfly, I reckoned it a blessing. But they seem to have eaten themselves out of prosperity, for there have not been nearly so many since, and this year the greenfly flourished with never an enemy in sight.

So do the flies in the wood. When I go out to take the dogs, there is a threatening black cloud that settles on any unprotected patch of skin. The more one swipes at them, to flatten them or drive them off, the more reinforcements take their place. They crawl on neck and hands – and my bald pate, if I neglect to protect it with my customary cap. They dance in front of my eyes more dizzily than the liverish spots that haunt the morning after. Short of enveloping oneself in a cloud of insecticide spray, which might be as lethal to me as to them, I know no way of quelling their attacks. So I put up with them.

My friends seem to be physically incapable of similar endurance. They flail their arms, faster than the sails of a windmill in a hurricane, which soon exhausts them but does nothing to the flies. They call down

27

curses on the buzzing wings, which simply makes them buzz harder in reply. They swathe their heads in bracken, without effect, while I wander on, lying that they never bother me.

They do, of course, but not nearly as much as they did. I long since decided that it was vital either to get used to them and make the best of things – or pack up going into the wood during the summer months. This would, of course, be unthinkable, for my wanderings there are among my greatest pleasures.

When I tried all the worthless recommended cures – and some I devised for myself – I realised that flies were something I had to live with. Then it dawned on me that, although they landed on my flesh and annoyed me by crawling about, they didn't actually bite. There were no lumps of irritation, as happens when the assailants are mosquitoes.

So when I escort some stranger round the wood, I put on an air of stoical indifference. The more my guests flap about and duck and squirm, the less notice I take. When I am told that the flies in my wood are intolerable, I ask, 'What flies?' I have got so accustomed to the flies that they mean little more than raindrops which I can ignore in order to appreciate the wood's pleasures.

One evening recently, I went into the wood towards dusk and, for some reason that I don't understand, the flies had all congregated at tree-top level so that, for once, they had forsaken their provocative ways. At first, I seriously thought that there was a squadron of Air Force fighter planes approaching in the distance. There was a continuous, loud, high-pitched buzzing in every direction high overhead. There must have been literally millions of woodland flies droning a dirge that drowned out lesser sounds. Since they were all so high, it was possible to stand and listen for minutes on end without a single insect coming into the attack. And, when I did eventually go out of the wood into an open glade, there were even more flies, though this time at ground level.

Not the small strident brutes that visitors so much dislike, but huge long-legged beasties which flew silently. They were daddy longlegs, or crane flies to the boffins, and they were at ground level because the females were all intent on laying eggs just under the surface of the sward. These will hatch out into leather jackets, small leathery grubs which do a lot of damage to the grass, making it go yellow and lifeless.

They are killed by farmers with chemical insecticides which, unfortunately, slaughter a lot of innocent insects along with the guilty. I shan't spray our glade, though, and the result will be a feast for the birds when the eggs the daddy (and mummy?) longlegs were laying incubate and hatch.

It is an example of the fact that there are nearly always two ways of looking at things. If you don't like creepie-crawlies, the Year of the Ladybird must have been sheer hell. But, if you were a keen gardener, and hate greenfly, the ladybirds did you nothing but good. In the same way, this year, the Year of the Flies, is worse than purgatory if they irritate you to death. But if you're a bird, or if, like me, you like birds, then this year has provided a glut of succulent food and the birds you like should be in for a bonanza. So I put up with the flies in our wood with a good grace!

7. Alice Sees Through Tessa's Eyes

A few years ago, I had a marvellous summer doing the things I enjoy most and working with people with similar interests. It is true that I was working for the hardest boss I know, but as that was myself and I got paid for what I did (and didn't get paid unless I produced something!), I was not complaining.

A good deal of my time was taken up with the TV series 'It's a Dog's Life' (*see also* No. 3) where I met a wide variety of owners. One Irish greyhound trainer had obviously kissed the Blarney stone and the chaps – and women! – at the gundog trial paid so little attention to the day-long sheeting rain that I reckoned their mothers were mermaids. But of all the delightful people that I met, Alice takes first prize. She had a bubbling sense of humour, the resilience of so many Cockneys and the courage of a lion.

Alice was sixty-eight and had been blind since she was four and had never had a dog in her life for the simple reason that she lived in homes where pets were not allowed. Her beloved budgie was the nearest she had got to animal ownership. However, when she began to get on in years, she was allocated an old people's flat in London and the authorities fixed her up with one on the ground floor with a patch of garden where she could have let the dog out – if she had had one!

So Alice applied for a guide dog and I first caught up with her when we were making a programme about training blind people and guide dogs to work together. There is a lot more to it than you might think. All you have to do to train a hound or a gundog is to pick one that has been selectively bred for the job and then to channel his natural instincts to suit your purpose. Chasing quarry is instinctive for hounds that hunt by sight, like greyhounds and whippets, so that if you arrange an 'artificial' quarry in the form of a mechanical hare, and pull it round a track a little faster than the dogs can run, you are in business for a greyhound race. Foxhounds and gundogs naturally use their noses to find their quarry,

A beautiful guide dog with its very fortunate owner

so that it is relatively straightforward to persuade them to go into partnership with you for the sport of your choice if you happen to like hunting or shooting.

Most guide dogs have the same instincts, for the majority of them are labrador retrievers. But, if they were piloting their blind owners across a busy street and took off after a cat or ran amok in a pet shop, they would be less than ideal for the job! Training guide dogs is therefore a specialist business where the first thing is to subdue their natural instincts and persuade them not only to do unnatural things but actually to enjoy doing them. The object of our programme was to go behind the scenes to discover precisely how this is done.

It is an expensive process, for the beginning has to be selective breeding as scientific and careful as for any champion hound or gundog. When the puppy is weaned, it has to go away to live in an ordinary home where it can be taught the civilised behaviour of a good house dog and get used to busy town life before its formal training can even begin. Then it has to go to a guide dog training centre where it spends months learning the intricate drill it will need to know before piloting its eventual blind owner on its own initiative. This is not funded by the Welfare State but paid for by voluntary subscriptions, raised with love by thousands of enthusiasts.

I was at the training centre when a new intake of blind owners arrived to do a four-week course, aimed at teaching them how to take over the fully trained dogs. The prospective owners, Alice amongst them, waited in the privacy of their own rooms to meet, for the first time, the dogs which would share life with them, for better or worse, through good tempers and foul and sad times and happy, for years to come. It was an emotional and moving experience to be privileged to witness such meetings. Some owners, like Alice, craved a companion to share their loneliness as much as a workmate to endow them with mobility and independence. Those who failed to get in tune with the dog would have to go home without one and manage as before.

I had immense admiration for Alice, who was game enough to start life afresh at her time of life, and we struck up an immediate friendship.

'Don't put the mockers on me,' she used to say if I pulled her leg too hard – she immediately pulled mine even harder.

However often she was asked to repeat an exercise, she was always cheerful, trying even harder next time. She loved her dog so much that she found it went against the grain to boss her, and we often wondered who was in charge, Alice or Tessa. Never having had a dog before, she had to start right at the beginning, learning to groom and feed and provide elementary care for her.

The other new owners were just as nice, so that it seemed unfair that we, who had no disability but all the advantages, could do so little for them. The end of the course came and the great day arrived when, for the first time, they would be launched into the busy streets of Reading at peak shopping time, with no one to rely on but their dogs. Alice and her friends took their courage in one hand and the harness of their dogs in the other and set out on their great adventure into the unknown with supreme confidence in their dogs.

8.   A Robin Has Something To Sing About

It may seem odd to live in a nature reserve and yet to get excited about a robin. We had more than forty herons' nests this year, green and spotted woodpeckers, tree-creepers and woodcock and gold-crested wrens. But standing out from all the rarities, nothing has given me greater pleasure than the cock robin, singing his heart out in a tree not five yards from my study window!

Not that it is particularly melodious. The poor fellow has only just come through the moult and nothing takes it out of a bird more than when he has to drop all his feathers and grow a new crop in the space of a few weeks. The sheer physical strain of such rapid growth makes great demands on stamina which is one of the main reasons why birdsong almost ceases in August and part of September. When the new feathers are through and shining with health, birds begin to feel like women with party hats that have drained their resources. They make a bit of a song about it to convince themselves that all the hassle was worth while.

Our robin is a bit like that. He is not yet entirely sold on the notion that his new outfit is all that it is cracked up to be. So, to put a brave face on it, he is perched on top of the prunus tree piping a reedy, almost experimental little song, just as small boys thrust their hands into their pockets and whistle to persuade themselves that they are not afraid in the dark. Later on, as he grows more confident, the notes will thicken up into a full-blooded tune, though it is not the hymn of praise romantic writers try to make us believe. It will then be more a war cry, roared in hate at any other robin that has the cheek to trespass on his territory.

It is not only the robin's song that fills my ears with delight – I am only too pleased that he is here at all. Most seasons we have lots of them but, for the last few months, in spite of such a wide variety of relative rarities, robins have been conspicuous by their absence. It is easy to notice when a bird arrives, far harder to pinpoint exactly when he is not there. Most seasons there is a robin's nest or so around the yard or in the hedge-bank along the edge of the garden. At the back of the tractor shed, there is a brick out of the wall that just gives the sort of cranny that must seem as if it was specially built to accommodate a nest. This summer, none of them has been inhabited. I have not found a single robin's nest about the place. There may, of course, have been several I haven't found, but I don't think so because we haven't seen any fledglings either.

Predators are probably the cause. There are a fair few tawny owls around and certainly too many foxes. It might seem odd to link foxes to the disappearance of so small a bird, but the robins frequently nest on the ground or very low and are just as tasty as pheasants or partridges, though it might need more for a satisfying meal! In addition to the several pairs of tawny owls, we have a pair of sparrow-hawks, and there's always a weasel or two. One weasel got into a tit box, ate the youngsters, and was then too fat to get back through the hole.*

Much as I like weasels, I did give him a one-way ticket, but I have seen a stoat in the garden recently and haven't made up my mind whether to put down a tunnel trap for him. We have far too many rabbits and, as stoats are the best natural control on their numbers, there are powerful arguments for leaving well alone in the hopes that he will help to stem their population explosion. On the other hand, I shot a stoat in the act of killing one of my Christmas cockerels a year or so ago, and I do not want an encore!

It raises the whole question of predators and conservation. From a distance, on other people's land, it is easy to be smug and generous and say that it is wrong to control any predators and that foxes and stoats and magpies and carrion crows have as much right to be left alone as songbirds. But if the same do-gooders get a rat in the coal-shed, a mouse in the kitchen or a wasp-nest in the compost heap, they are soon squealing for the pest destruction officer. It's the old story that a weed is a wild flower in the wrong place!

Some people who criticise gamekeepers for killing everything but game – and I admit to being among their loudest critics – are quite prepared to spray their roses or cabbages with insecticide to control the caterpillars without a thought for the blue tits that may die from an

---

* *see Country Wise, page 176*

overdose of poison swallowed with the insects that are their natural diet. It is dangerously easy to get all steamed up at the very idea of killing 'nice' creatures, like pretty grey squirrels or graceful stoats, while 'nasty' creatures, like rats and caterpillars do not rate a second thought despite the fact that, left to themselves, the caterpillars would eventually turn into gorgeous butterflies.

My own belief is that there is no such thing as the 'balance of nature'. Every abnormally dry or wet season changes it. If you get a 'good' year for ladybirds, it is usually because there has been a good year for greenflies, their staple diet. If we plant more woodland or grub out more hedges or use more agricultural chemicals, it will have profound effects on a whole chain of creatures quite unconnected with farming or forestry. So I try to manage my wood for the benefit of creatures that would otherwise be under pressure. Sparrow hawks were getting rare, so I regarded small birds that feed in the paddock as a crop to feed them. But I got tough with magpies and crows that could have tipped the balance too far. The welcome reappearance of my robins is a yardstick that the plan is practical and balancing out reasonably well.

9.   Free To Come And Go

Jack, the baby muntjac deer I reared on the bottle three years ago* is now full grown, though no bigger than a fox. When he was growing up, I was given a wild doe that had been injured in an accident, but although she recovered fully, she never grew tame and spends most of her time skulking in deep cover because it has not yet dawned on her that nobody wishes to do her any harm. The other doe, Minnie, is quite different.* She was found abandoned in the snow last winter and grew up in my study to be friendly with the dogs. She is as vain and affectionate – and greedy – as most beautiful females of any species so that any visitor who rattles a bowl of corn is immediately added to her list of friends for life and everybody adores her.

All three of them have lived happily in an enclosure by my study window where there is thick cover for them to lie up, varied grazing and an acre or so of space. Although this is theoretically ample for their needs, I am never happy about keeping wild creatures in any form of captivity. I should have let them go long ago if I had not known what inveterate wanderers muntjac deer are. They are really natives of China and their ancestors were brought over at the end of the last century by the Duke of Bedford to add to the collection of deer he kept in his park at Woburn. Some of them escaped and settled in the surrounding countryside where they bred and increased because it obviously suited them very well. They were such natural wanderers that they gradually spread out over the surrounding country and are now quite common as far north as Warwickshire. The conurbation of Birmingham and the Black Country act as a barrier to their progress, but that does not stop them trying! Most years an odd one or two break through Birmingham's outer defences and get into the suburbs where they are hounded by the local dogs until they are either caught, run over, or rescued.

Some of these fugitives have been sent to me in the past, so that I can liberate them in my wood to give them a fresh chance in life. They are

* *see Country Wise*

37

such natural wanderers that they have soon disappeared and I never knew what happened to them. So I have kept my tame ones in the enclosure more for their own safety than for my enjoyment.

A few months ago I put up several hundred yards of deer-proof fence to allow the wood where the herons nest to thicken up with cover because, while the fallow deer are allowed free access, they nip off any young shoots before they can grow into trees. This fence serves the double purpose of dividing the main part of my wood from the big wood outside so that it is now a sensible calculated risk to let the muntjacs out

The muntjac fawn amongst the daffodils

of their paddock with a fair chance that they will stay around. They have now had their complete freedom for a full week – and we still see them every day.

It is a pretty nail-biting time for, if they do stray away, there is every chance that they will be shot by some trigger-happy 'sportsman' or be killed by a pack of hounds. I have had to take the decision of giving them complete liberty, with all the natural pleasure that that entails, but also with the knowledge that they may come to a violent and sticky end if things don't work out. Rearing any small animal on the bottle entails close physical contact a minimum of four times a day for half an hour or so, and I find it impossible not to become personally involved. It is natural to grow fond of any helpless creature that is so dependent on you. But death from old age is very rare among wild creatures because such a high proportion are killed by predators (including man!) or die in territorial fights, as badgers often do.

So my three muntjac are really in no greater peril than they would have been if they had grown up in the wild and, so long as they stay in my wood, their chances are exceptional.

When I made a hole in the enclosure fence, Minnie, the young doe, popped out within half an hour and disappeared in the wood. The little buck came next and disappeared in the opposite direction, but the wild doe took three days to venture beyond the enclosure which she obviously regarded as her territory. They now pop in and out quite freely, coming 'home' at dusk to gorge on the wheat I put in a pile for them every night. What does puzzle me – and I have no idea of the answer – is that they go off in different directions into the wood and lie up in thick cover. As soon as I see one moving in one part of the wood, it is a fair bet that the other two will appear, as if by magic, from several hundred yards away.

Whatever it is that sparks them into action, the result is that they frequently come toddling 'home' down different woodland rides to meet up in their own enclosure as if summoned by a dinner gong that none but they can hear. So I live in hopes that they will continue to regard our wood as home and stay in safety to enthral us for many years to come.

NOTE: *see also* Nos. 18 and 21

10. Prey For This Killer . . .

A reader telephoned in great distress to say that a kestrel hawk was killing blue tits and other small birds which came to feed on her bird-table. It dived into the bush where they were perching, yanked them out and flew away with them. Should she get the pest officer to destroy it? Or how could she do so herself?

It never does to take such stories at face value. I happen to know that kestrels catch most of their prey by hovering above it and suddenly pouncing. I also know that the favourite diet of kestrels is not small birds, but the voles, mice and beetles that creep about in thick cover, like the grass along motorway verges. This one seemed to be acting out of character but, since it is never safe to generalise with wildlife, I asked her to describe the hawk she had seen.

'A slatey-blue bird,' she said, 'something like a cuckoo. And it dived at the bush like a rocket.'

That clinched it. Her small birds' attacker was not a kestrel but a sparrow-hawk. So I explained that kestrels were harmless birds which preyed on the mice and beetles that do damage to agricultural and garden crops and that sparrow-hawks are still comparatively rare as they are only just recovering from near extinction caused by eating small birds that were dying from chemical poisons used to control pests on the land.* She was really very lucky that a sparrow-hawk had decided to feed in her garden! The explosion that followed demonstrated the difference between naturalists, like me, and more conventional bird lovers.

She said she couldn't care less whether sparrow-hawks were rare to the point of extinction. The small birds in her garden relied on her for hospitality and no brute of a hawk was going to slaughter them if she could help it. I asked her if she'd got a cat and, if so, whether that ever took any of her birds.

'That's different,' she said. 'And, anyway, he only catches sparrows.'

* *see Country Scene*, page 187

Sparrow-hawks are rare enough to be on the list of protected species

I then explained that the blue tits probably had at least two nests a year and reared eight or ten from each. If something didn't feed on them, there would be a population explosion of blue tits, which might be very nice but would soon account for all the available food so that the rest would starve. However attractive she thought they were, Mother Nature regarded them as a crop, from which the surplus could form the diet of predatory birds like sparrow-hawks. It wasn't what she wanted to hear so I took the argument a stage further.

I asked if she had any thrushes in her garden. She had, and said their song gave her delight all summer and their beautiful spotted waistcoats brought pleasure in winter. They spent hours a day digging the worms out of her lawn, thereby saving her sweeping away the ugly worm casts.

'Why is it all right for the thrushes to catch the worms that enjoy the hospitality of your lawn,' I asked, 'when it is wrong for the sparrow-hawks to enjoy the hospitality of your bird-table, where they probably think you provide a plenteous feast of blue tits?'

It got me nowhere. Sentiment overrides reason with so much wildlife. Deer are 'beautiful' – so it is wrong to hunt them. Rats are 'dirty' – so no fate is too bad. Both views can't be right.

Sparrow-hawks have bred in our wood two years running and I see the old birds hunting for food to feed their young quite often in the summer. In winter, I have the same experience as the reader who complained. There is a thick, prickly berberis bush on the edge of the lawn, where a flock of sparrows roost. Sometimes, at dusk, the hawk appears, as if by magic, dives right into the heart of the bush, and is out with a sparrow before his fellows realise what has happened. Now our sparrows raid the corn I put down for the poultry – so I don't mind. I am illogical too.

Gamekeepers, who are paid to rear pheasants, feel as strongly about sparrow-hawks taking pheasant poults as ladies who keep bird-tables when they see their feathered guests disappear. But most of the nature lovers go up in smoke at the idea of a keeper killing a predator in spite of the fact that they are ready to send for the pest officer to destroy the same hawk for a similar 'crime' at their bird-table. Fortunately, sparrow-hawks are rare enough to be on the list of protected species and it is against the law for keepers, pest officers or ladies who keep bird-tables to destroy them. If their numbers increased to pest pro-portions, as carrion crows and magpies have, my hand would be against them too. But while hawks are comparatively rare and in need of protection, I am delighted that the law is on their side.

11. Exit In A Cloud Of Smoke

When I was working in a factory, I was fairly gadget-minded. So the theft of some pigeons which I kept in a field across the road was a sort of challenge. I fixed a blank shotgun cartridge in a heavy steel hinge so that the cartridge exploded if the hinge was swung over centre. Then I attached a piece of cotton to the pen door so that anyone opening the door without first disconnecting the cotton swung the hinge off balance. There were no pellets in the blank cartridge, which left room for about twice as much powder as normal. The din it made, in the still of the night, was enough to awaken the dead.

The next time the thief called, I have no doubt that he crept up to the pen as stealthily as a shadow and inched the door quietly open, to be greeted by a blinding flash and shattering explosion. He would have no way of knowing whether it was a harmless automatic alarm gun or the irate owner taking a pot shot and missing him by inches. Nor did he stay to find out. There was no doubt that he left in a hurry, because I found the seat of his pants on the barbed wire fence next morning.

I had got the idea from the keeper friends of my childhood who used alarm guns extensively in their pheasant coverts. Their predecessors in the last century had used alarm guns that fired live cartridges instead of blanks, which were probably even more effective though they were made illegal because of the havoc they caused to guilty and innocent alike.

The last few days before Christmas are still about the most critical in a keeper's year because poachers find a ready market for their spoils. All over the country vigilant keepers will have set their alarm guns with cottons stretched across gaps and woodland rides that poachers are likely to cross on their way to find roosting birds. But that is only half the job. The object of the exercise is not only to scare the poachers off. Good keepers want to catch them. It is obvious that an intruder letting off an alarm gun doesn't hang around waiting to be caught. He legs it for home as hard as he can. This may prove to be his undoing because the keepers will also have stretched strong fencing wires about a foot above the ground at intervals across the woodland rides. These wires will have been placed by prominent trees that are obvious to those in the know but strangers will have no way of locating them in the dark.

Hitting a trip wire flat out in the dark is as good a way as I know of taking a toss that will knock the wind out of your sails and leave you vulnerable to arrest without much struggle. Modern keepers, however, have more sophisticated methods. Some of the best equipped have walkie-talkie radios and binoculars that can 'see' in the dark. These modern binocular field-glasses are quite incredible. A year or two ago, I was invited to do a series of TV programmes which observed and filmed badgers in complete darkness. Infra-red light is not perceptible to the human (or badger!) eye. So cameras had been set up overlooking a badger sett which was 'lit' by infra red rays that left an image with the camera but were invisible to the badgers and us.

The programme worked fine but, before we could begin, it had been

The poacher's deterrent: an anti-poacher gun photographed at
Cambridge Folk Museum

necessary to do a great deal of observation to decide precisely where the cameras would be most effective. The observations had been made through these binoculars, working as light intensifiers, which really can see in almost pitch blackness. Some of these devices can be coupled to a camera, either TV or still, or, in the case of the armed services, to the sights of a firearm. On a moonless winter night, it is possible to see what is going on as clearly as with the naked eye in broad daylight.

The makers sent me a catalogue illustrating just what their products would do, not only as an aid in detecting the activities of poachers, but for watching badgers and foxes and other nocturnal creatures, which is more to my personal taste. The only snag is the price. I fear that even Santa Claus won't stump up about £1000 for my amusement, so I have passed the catalogue on to a keeper friend whose boss has more money than sense. If the ruse works, I may be able to borrow these superb night-glasses for nothing. But, to be on the safe side, I've plastered the wood with bangers and trip wires to give uninvited guests a welcome.

12. Catalogue Of Death

A friend who farms in Shropshire has started a bleak New Year. He had a grand corn harvest last autumn, and managed to cultivate his stubbles and sow his winter wheat exceptionally well. He visualised himself laughing all the way to the bank again later this year. The grains sprouted and the young corn positively leaped away until he began to worry that it was too far forward and might be flattened and damaged by winter snow or frost. So he contemplated turning the sheep on to it to bite it down a little so it could sprout again in spring. He needn't have bothered – just before Christmas it began to wilt.

Close examination soon revealed the cause. His crop had been afflicted by a plague of slugs. So my friend referred to the Farmers' Bible, which rejoices in the title of *Approved Products for Farmers and Growers*. It is a catalogue of chemicals, issued annually by the Ministry of Agriculture, Fisheries and Food, listing the substances the Ministry recommends for the destruction of almost every conceivable pest that can afflict farm or garden crops. Unfortunately, the remedies the Ministry prescribes can be equally fatal to countless birds, beasts and insects that don't happen to be pests. The diet acclaimed as the control for slugs and snails is a substance called metaldehyde. It is the same stuff gardeners buy as slug pellets.

To be fair to the boffins at the Ministry, their approved guide does advise that containers should be kept tightly closed and away from children, domestic animals and livestock. It goes on to say that it is harmful to fish, dangerous to game and that poultry should be kept off land where it has been used for at least seven days.

Farmers are a funny lot. Like the rest of us, they too often read the bits they want to know and ignore the rest. As soon as my pal saw that metaldehyde was recommended by the men from the ministry as the answer to slugs, he dashed off and bought a bag and dumped it in the gadget that fits on the back of his tractor to broadcast seed or patent manure. This consists of a cone-shaped container that dribbles its contents out on to a spinning horizontal plate that distributes anything falling on it in a wide arc behind the tractor. He drove off round his slug-infested crop, leaving a fine layer of slug pellets behind him.

If he had bothered to read the instructions thoroughly, he would have left Sam, his favourite dog, at home. Sam was his faithful friend who followed wherever he went as surely as his shadow. So Sam tagged on behind when he went to the wheatfield to deal with the slugs. Unfortunately, metaldehyde is not only attractive to slugs. Sam also discovered its attractions and, before my friend realised what was happening, Sam was dead.

Any real dog lover would have felt the same about it. It ruined my friend's Christmas and has sent him into the New Year feeling very low. His guilty conscience hammers home the lesson that it is nobody's fault but his own that his trusting companion died a premature and painful death. I don't happen to agree that it was entirely his own fault.

Of course the farmer should have read the label and followed the instructions more carefully. Sam would be alive today if he had. Of course he should have kept his poultry away and made certain the surplus didn't fall in his goldfish pond. But what about the wild animals and birds that lived in the area? They can't read and write and have no way of knowing that it is dangerous for them to go on the land for the next seven days. Some of the substances recommended in the Ministry guide warn that stock must be kept clear not for seven days but *eight weeks*!

Some say that the world contains a potentially starving human race and that we must grow the maximum food at all costs. To hell with wildlife that suffers in the process. To hell with Sam the dog, I suppose they would add. I concede we need as much food as we can grow and we cannot put the clock back. But I believe there are limits beyond which it is immoral to go. What sort of society are we to allow such indiscriminate poisons to be broadcast on our land and to pay bureaucrats, out of our taxes, to recommend the stuff? Surely, if chemists are brilliant enough to concoct such devastating brews, it is not beyond the wit of man to make them selective for the pests they are designed to kill? Surely slug pellets could be made to taste too foul for dogs and wild animals and birds to eat? If they can't, the Ministry should delete them from their list until they can. And the only way I know of achieving that is by the pressure of public opinion continually nudging MPs to air the matter in Parliament.

13.   Mini Hunters Get A Maxi Feast

A chyme of dandy dogs hunted in full cry across our lawn this week. They didn't stick together as close as a well-trained pack of fox hounds wound have done but, since it is impossible to train the hounds of the fairies, this is not surprising.

In case you don't know what dandy dogs look like, they are a gorgeous russet-brown with white bellies. Their legs are short, for they stand no more than an inch from the ground and they measure almost as far as a man can span from tip to tail. Before you reach for the classified directory to send the hunt saboteurs round to our house to disrupt our next lawn meet, I should tell you that you would be wasting your time. Although countryfolk call the fairy hounds that hunted across our lawn dandy dogs, naturalists call them weasels!

Round the edge of the garden we have a ha-ha, or dry moat, to stop the deer jumping in and munching my wife's treasured flowers. This ha-ha is about five feet deep with a fairly gentle slope down from the paddock side and an almost vertical wall to stop deer jumping up from the bottom.

There are all sorts of nooks and crannies behind this wall and bank voles have dug a maze of tunnels there from which they emerge at dusk to chobble the short turf at the edge of the lawn. They are delightful, rounded, cosy little creatures that remind me of the mice in story books when I was a kid and we enjoy watching them sitting on their haunches, holding a blade of grass between delicate forepaws as nimbly as a squirrel eating nuts. Unfortunately for the voles, they are among the favourite items on a weasel's diet sheet.

Weasels get their grub the hard way. They don't sit and wait for it to wander within pouncing distance, as a lazy cat would do. They hunt by scent and sight and run it down when it tries to escape. We saw the whole drama on the lawn the other day. Or to be more precise, we came in after the first scene of the first act. I first noticed movement out of the corner of my eye as a russet brown body popped out of a hole at the top of the ha-ha like a cork out of a bottle of champagne. It was a weasel not much bigger than a man's thumb. Easy to see how impressionable countryfolk would think he was just the right size for fairies to use for the sport of hunting. In his jaws he was carrying a fat vole that he had just winkled out of a hole at the back of the ha-ha. He was immediately followed by another weasel and then a third in line astern, also carrying their furry booty.

Michael Clark's hand-reared weasel knows a good book when he sees one!

They all disappeared at the bottom of the hedge but, long before they could have had time to eat their quarry, they returned and started to scour the holes that they had just emerged from. It is obvious why countrymen call them dandy dogs, because they spread out, as a pack of hounds would 'feather the line', using their sensitive noses to locate another bank vole. Their action is very like a tiny rocking horse so that they undulated over the ground as a pack of dogs would hunt and within seconds another vole had bolted for safety – but never reached whatever sanctuary he had been aiming for. I have seen several weasels hunting in a pack – or chyme – like this before, but never in January.

Bitch weasels normally have two litters a year, one in spring and the other in autumn. They nest either in holes in the ground or, sometimes, in hollow trees or crevices in the stonework of walls or buildings. After five weeks, the young emerge and they are among the most agile and playful creatures I have ever seen. But life is not all a game. Their play is really a rehearsal of the serious business of catching food and their mother leads them off to well-stocked hunting grounds where there should be no difficulty in finding the mice or voles that weasels love to eat. When they are very young, they tag on behind mum, head-to-tail, so close they could almost be mistaken for a snake. They follow while she finds her quarry, hunts it and kills it, allowing the whole litter to share the sacrificial feast.

When they get a little older and know from experience what it is all about, they spread out instead of simply following blindly, and this is when the country description of a chyme of dandy dogs fits them precisely. As soon as they can look after themselves, their mother drives them off to find fresh territory for themselves. She will attack them ruthlessly if they come back to trespass on her patch – it is vital that she doesn't kill the goose that lays the golden egg by killing too many voles before she has her second litter in autumn. These in turn, she will drive off before winter to look after themselves.

All winter she lives a solitary life and will attack her mate, her own litter or trespassing strangers. So I don't know what three dandy dogs were doing together when I saw them hunting on our lawn. What I do know is that they fired the primitive hunting instinct in me and that I was as thrilled to watch them as any dyed-in-the-wool hunting man!

14.   Deadly Cockles For Tea

During the winter of 1979/80, thousands of birds, mostly sea birds and waders, were found dead on the shores of the Mersey estuary. The mystery of their death has not yet been solved. All that is known, so far, is that they appear to have died from some sort of lead poisoning, though where the lead came from is not yet clear. Most people jumped to the conclusion that some factory along Merseyside had been polluting the river with poisonous waste but, if this is so, investigations have not yet pinpointed the culprit.

Knots feeding along the estuary bed

The natural food of many of the dead birds consists of the small shellfish and worms that thrive in the mud of rivers and estuaries and the remains of these creatures salvaged from the victims at post mortem have shown an excessive proportion of lead in their bodies. It appears that some of these simple forms of life, which live in mud, can actually concentrate the lead that passes through their bodies when they are feeding. Instead of killing them, the lead builds up into a positive arsenal of poison so that the birds or animals eating them may die of secondary poisoning. Not a healthy area to collect cockles for your tea! But if the river is not being polluted by lead upstream, where does the lead come from that is getting into the bodies of small shellfish which, in turn, are poisoning the birds?

Modern river boards are obsessed with the urge to dredge the rivers under their control till they become mere drains, sluicing water to the sea. All over the country these men with tidy little minds are ripping out the trees from river banks so that their machines can dredge up the river beds, converting lovely stretches into geometric sewers. Water, which has always been absorbed into the soil to enrich the land with springs and streams, is now flushed away to waste for the sake of saving a few marginal acres of marsh – which is already one of our most precious shrinking types of country.

One of the reasons that river boards are so besotted with their craze to dredge is that the mechanical equipment they use is now so expensive that the outlay of public money can only be justified if it is employed full-time. Like computers, such machines are too often the masters of the men who use them. They soon complete the tasks for which they were acquired so that work has to be found to keep them employed or the cost will prove prohibitive.

One theory to account for the death of the Merseyside birds is that modern dredging equipment is so efficient that it is disturbing mud which has lain dormant for years and the lead waste that is now being churned up was spewed out of some bygone factory long before regulations were tightened up. Perhaps the sins of our fathers are being visited on us.

Within a few miles of this mayhem, the Dee estuary has just been bought as a nature reserve to save it from being drained by a foreign buyer. It is one of the most important wintering grounds for many species of ducks and geese and waders, and its loss would have been catastrophic. Public awareness of our heritage of wildlife has sharpened out of all proportion in my lifetime. When I was at school, I was considered rather eccentric because I belonged to the 'Bug Soc.', which was the disparaging term for the natural history society. We were thought rather wet because we preferred bird-nesting or looking for butterflies to playing cricket in summer, and anyone who could summon up enthusiasm for wild flowers was suspected of having a feminine streak.

Modern youths are proud to wear the Young Ornithologists badge or sport a tie with badgers' heads because they are members of their local county naturalists' trust. Yet in spite of all the pressure that conservationists apply, we are killing more wild birds with oil slicks or farm chemicals or, now, the mysterious lead poisoning along the Mersey estuary, than the worst gamekeepers in my grandfather's time.

Bureaucrats have exterminated thousands of badgers in the West Country and innocent gardeners in suburbia feed birds on their bird-tables all winter and poison them with slug pellets and greenfly spray all summer. I know of only one way to halt the slide and that is by the weight of public opinion. Both bureaucrats and big business are susceptible to parliamentary votes which can result in new laws. At the moment, when one industrial chemist produces a spray that will kill a pest in ten minutes, his competitor is briefed to produce an answer that will kill the same pest in one minute less. Public opinion could limit approval to substances that are less dangerous, even if slightly less efficient, and it could restrict operations such as dredging until the results of disturbing dangerous waste have been sensibly calculated. If nobody acts, we have only ourselves to blame if the next unexplained catastrophe is not limited to birds.

15. Return Of The Nuthatches

Ten years ago I described the disappearance of redstarts and nut-hatches from our wood.* When we arrived at Goat Lodge in 1964, both species were common and redstarts, which spend the summer here but migrate, like swallows in winter, actually nested behind a crevice in the garage. They have backsides as red as robins' breasts and catch flying insects as nimbly as flycatchers, but they have become less common all over the country. This is partly because of droughts in North Africa and partly because of the uncivilised behaviour of continental 'sportsmen' who massacre tens of thousands of birds on migration every year.

Nuthatches are different. They do not migrate and are natives of English woodlands with a delightful, limpid call that draws the attention of the most unmusical ears. It is a sort of wolf-whistle that might convince the spottiest teenager that she was being given the come-hither by some romantic stranger. So, when we came, the evidence of our ears left us in no doubt that we shared the wood with nuthatches. This was quickly confirmed by their appearance on the fat we hang above the bird-table. Nuthatches love fat. They are about the size of kingfishers and, though their colours are not so brilliant, they always remind me of them. The upper parts are blue-grey, though much duller than the flamboyant sheen of kingfishers. The throat and belly are buff and the flanks a lovely chestnut. There is a distinctive, broad black stripe from the top of the bill, through the eye to the shoulder. As often happens with chauvinist good-lookers, nuthatches are swash-buckling brigands who tip everyone else off the fat we put out for tits and woodpeckers.

Or, to be more precise, they did tip their rivals off the fat because, just ten years ago, the nuthatches simply disappeared from our woods where, so the oldest locals told us, they had been common longer than the greyest-headed grand-dad could remember.

So I lamented their disappearance and asked other bird-watchers if

* *see Country Scene*, page 98

54

they had noticed the same thing. Friends up to six or seven miles away said that their bird fat was now patronised only by tits, woodpeckers and the ubiquitous starlings. But I was never able to get any confirmation of it from the scientific boffins who look down on us amateurs and always describe themselves as ornithologists. I found nothing in the literature that proliferates in such distinguished circles. So I came to the conclusion that a major change in the character of our local woodland was probably the cause.

Nuthatches love native English woods like oak, birch, sycamore and ash. They love hazelnuts and beechmast and they have an engaging way of cracking them. I have often seen them carry a nut to a tree with the right-sized crevice in the bark, wedge the nut fast, till it is held as in a vice, and then hammer it until they split it with their powerful bills. Like me, they are not in love with soft woods and the Forestry Commission had planted about a thousand acres of pine trees over our boundary, leaving our hard wood isolated at one corner. Perhaps the local nuthatches had found a more attractive habitat now that their

The typical hanging posture of a nuthatch

feeding ground had been so reduced by unpalatable pines? Whatever the cause, we grew used to their absence and almost forgot that they were a regular attraction until a decade ago.

Imagine my delight, therefore, when I was brought up short one morning recently by the most seductive wolf whistle. I thought at first that it was a starling doing one of his impersonations. The cock starling that nests in the tractor shed obviously spends his holiday on the edge of wild moorland or beside a muddy estuary, because he mimics the plaintive cry of curlews more accurately than Mike Yarwood copies the pipe-smoking man who used to be Prime Minister.* And another starling is a dead ringer for the green woodpecker or yaffle. But the wolf whistle that halted me in my tracks was no counterfeit. It was the real thing, confirmed a moment later by the sight of a beautiful cock nuthatch hopping up and across and down the trunk of an oak tree with the grace of an Olympic athlete.

I followed him across the wood, hoping against hope that his mate would join him, but he was the only one I saw. So I came back to the house and moved the bird fat from its hook by the side of the window to a prunus tree half way between the house and the edge of the wood. I thought that if he had been reared in the depths of some isolated wood he might be a bit shy about risking getting too close to us. It may, of course, have been a chance excursion. Perhaps he had been scared by rowdy shooters, or his mate may have died so that it was necessary to mount an expedition into strange territory to find a fresh one. Or, with luck, there is a colony of survivors somewhere fairly near, which has thrived until it is getting overpopulated and the surplus has been forced to spill over into the surrounding countryside. In which case, I can promise them a warm welcome in our wood, with seclusion in summer and all the delicious fat they want in winter!

* *see Country Wise, page 52*

NOTE: A pair of nuthatches settled in the wood last winter, bred in the spring, so – with luck – we shall hear their wolf whistles as regular music again.

16. Walking Goes A Full Circle

Old countrymen tell tales of walking five or six miles to school and sometimes more than that to work. And, when I was a boy, I often helped a farmer from Little Bloxwich drive cattle to Lichfield to market. That is nine miles, as the crow flies, but cattle do not walk (or run) as the crow flies. For the first mile or so they are as skittish as carthorses turned out to grass. They dive through every open gate and leave hoof prints and worse on cossetted lawns and flower-beds. So we used to start at crack of dawn so that we could retrieve them and be safely on our way before irate owners could tumble out of bed to fill our ears with maledictions. Pedestrians and cyclists, who were jostled by our frisky brutes, were often equally narrow-minded!

About half way to Lichfield, a change set in. Left to themselves, cattle are not gluttons for exercise. They walk no further than is necessary to cram a load of lush herbage down them and then they settle down to enjoy it by chewing the cud. The cattle we drove to market were fat but not fit. When their initial exuberance wore off, our problem was not to stop them escaping up every open gateway but to keep them on the move at all. The pace may have been slower but the effort demanded from us was much more tiring. Modern farmers, who only have to drive their beasts up the ramp of a cattle truck, do not know they have been born.

We had bread and cheese and cider at one of Lichfield's many pubs and, since cattle droving is men's work, nobody queried our tender age! The only way back, apart from foot-slogging it, was by train to Walsall, tram to Bloxwich and walk the rest. So going nine miles was quite an adventure, to which spice was added by watching the beasts sold under the auctioneer's hammer. There was no way that we could have persuaded them to walk back home again, so my farmer friend had to take the best offer, which sharpened the incentive to watch the market trends and only to send his beasts in when the price was right. Now that

57

motor cars are regarded as necessities rather than luxuries, it is difficult to visualise just how the pace of life has altered since those days.

Every village was a tight-knit community and a very high percentage of the inhabitants was related because it was quite a problem to go courting several miles away when hours of work on the land were often six in the morning till six at night. Then, as now, cows had to be milked twice a day, seven days a week. Every hour of daylight was precious when land had to be ploughed a single furrow at a time by horses which had no power take-off or multi-speed gearbox. The pace of country living may have been slow but it never stopped till darkness fell.

Internal combustion engines altered all that. Motor cars have been common for as long as I can remember but my farmer friend from Little Bloxwich only had horses when I was growing up. His first tractor was a Ferguson, not very different from the one I still use in the wood, which is twenty-three years old and still going strong. But it was the arrival of motor cars that really changed the countryside. As farms became mechanised, wages increased so that it suddenly became possible for farm labourers to buy a little car and live in surrounding villages instead of in a cottage on the farm.

Farm cottages, when they came on the market, were often snapped up by townsfolk from miles around, sometimes as weekend cottages or sometimes as escapes from modern pressure from which the owners could commute to work. For the first time for generations, strangers popped up in every village and pressures from friends who wanted to join them persuaded the planners to allow village populations to expand by giving permission for many more houses to be built.

The common practice is to declare the centre of the village a conservation area, where the appearance must not be altered, and to site new houses, often jerrybuilt and as similar as hutches on an intensive rabbit farm, on new estates where they will not be noticed by casual passers-by.

The incomers, understandably attracted by the idea of escaping from the urban rat race, too often find that they have the worst of both worlds. Their houses are packed as close together as on any urban housing development so that the expected peace and privacy proves to be a mirage. Strangers monitor every move and visitor cats dig up their treasured garden plants, whilst commuting to work is more expensive and frustrating than ever it was before. Now there is an oil shortage and travel costs are daunting. Already the faint-hearted (or far-sighted?) are drifting back to the towns where they can live nearer to their work. It may soon be necessary to walk as much as our ancestors to enjoy life in the countryside again.

17.   Odds On The Newts

If I were a betting man, I'd lay heavy odds that the most unlikely story to hit the headlines recently came from Cheltenham racecourse. Some gullible reporter had been persuaded that the Cheltenham Gold Cup, shortly to be run, is threatened by a plague of newts in the water jump. And, if you swallow that, you will believe it is the punters, not the bookies, who make fortunes on the turf.

Perhaps he had a superstitious granny because I remember, when I was a boy, we did not call them newts, we called them wet efts or askers. The old grannies' tale, in those days, insisted that askers were very dangerous reptiles, closely related to dragons and, as everybody knows, dragons spit fire. If you don't believe that, have a look at any ancient picture of St George killing the dragon and you will see that spumes of fire and smoke are pouring out of the dragon's fearsome mouth. Newts are perfect miniatures of legendary dragons so simple country folk and credulous reporters can easily be persuaded that the habits of one are similar to the habits of the other.

I remember carrying a female crested newt, with her black, warty hide and glorious orange-yellow belly, into the classroom of my kindergarten and not only wringing screams of terror from the little girls but also the school ma'am, who should have known better. The belief is not confined to the backwoods of Staffordshire. In Switzerland, they have a species of salamander, which is very like a large newt (or little dragon) and they believe that it is born in the heart of a fire.

So no wonder the racegoers of Cheltenham have got the wind up. The mettlesome nags that are to be ridden over the water jump there might well shy and unseat their jockeys if dragons, even tiny monsters, reared their ugly heads and spat fire just as they were about to take off. Which would, of course, upset the odds. As a result, naturalists have been called in to collect the newts and transfer them to quieter ponds, which may well be safer for the newts as well as the horses. But I trust they will choose their ponds with care because I know of another superstition which claims that it is very dangerous for a horse to eat, or drink, a newt. I owe a great deal to them because it was my newts, more than any other creatures, that fired my love of natural history.

I spent hours, as a child, dredging in the swags or mining subsidence pools that lay in the fields around my home in Bloxwich. A friend once caught twenty, which she brought round, complete with a spherical goldfish bowl, as a present for my eighth birthday. My mother, who was not particularly keen on natural history, was even less enamoured with the score of tiny dragons writhing in the crystal water. But she could not very well make me spurn another child's present that she had spent so much of her time catching. Besides, the goldfish bowl was far more respectable than the jam jars in which I kept my minnows.

So the goldfish bowl fetched up as the centre decoration on our dining table and, for weeks, the whole family was entranced by the antics of

Common or smooth newts – safe from the horses

our amphibious guests. Their courtship dance was enthralling, for the gaudy coloured males swam in sinuous curves, embracing their mates as gracefully as competitors in a slow-motion tango. A female does not spawn out shapeless masses of eggs, as common frogs do. Her eggs are expelled in a single chain and she reaches down to separate the end egg and hold it gently in feet as delicate as a maiden's fingers. The egg is carefully wrapped in the leaf of a water plant, to make it invisible to hungry fish, and to enable the tadpole to develop undisturbed inside it, to hatch and grow into a tiny replica of its miniature dragon parents in due course.

My newts' table manners were their least attractive characteristic. I fed them on worms and their eyes were too often bigger than their stomachs. They gripped one end of their quarry in their jaws and gradually forced the worm down their gullets. Not unnaturally, the worms objected and often wriggled back to freedom, which the family, not being keen naturalists, considered bad manners at breakfast. Being hearty eaters, the newts triumphed in the end but their skins were not designed to grow to keep pace. So, at intervals, their skin split and was discarded complete, floating in the water as diaphanous as the night-dress of a bride.

If I were riding in the Cheltenham Gold Cup, I should dismount at the water jump and watch the newts.

18.   Experience Beats Book-learning

I find that when I am writing these chapters, I write for about five minutes in every hour – and look out of the window for fifty-five. This is not such a disastrous rate of productivity as you might think. Many of the things I write about happen while I am watching but I can find no reference to them in books on natural history.

I mentioned, for example, that I reared three tiny muntjac deer in an enclosure by the house, then gave them their freedom in the wood.* I was naturally anxious to know whether they would settle down here or wander off, because the books describe them as restless creatures that always seem to expect that the grass in the next field will be greener than anything they have experienced before.

The movement of the muntjac catches my eye when they cross an open ride and, as in our society, the females seem to lead and the old man tags on behind. The old doe is about as big as a fox, and not a very big fox at that. She trots along, with her head held so low that, in the distance, she reminds me of the gait of a hedgehog. Although they seem quite sociable little creatures, they often lie up and spend the day in different parts of the wood. But at intervals during the day, they come out into the open, graze or browse on leaves for a while, and then disappear to lie down to chew their cud and digest what they have harvested. When one decides to get up and go out foraging, the others seem to know by instinct, for they all appear, often in different woodland rides, within a minute or so of the first one showing up.

I have not been able to discover how they communicate with each other when they are several hundred yards apart and, if the experts who have written books about muntjac deer know the answer, they have kept it to themselves. What I have discovered, which the books don't mention either, is how they find each other when they do get on the

* *see* No. 9

63

move. When I am gazing vacantly out of my study window, the least movement catches my eye. One of the does will creep out of the thicket, take a few mouthfuls of food and usually disappear on the opposite side of the ride. This encourages my idleness so that I now have a reason, rather than an excuse, for giving my typewriter a rest.

When the buck appears, it is obvious that, for the moment, he is more interested in company than in food. He moves faster than his mates and his head does not just hang in the slovenly gait of a hedgehog. His nose is close to the ground, which he traverses in deliberate sweeps like a foxhound that has temporarily lost the scent of his quarry. It took a long time for this to dawn on me because I had been brought up to visualise deer as timid creatures, intent only on escaping from their enemies. The

The buck muntjac puts his nose down and hunts his mate's line

idea that they would follow a trail, like predatory hounds on the scent of their prey, never crossed my mind.

I now have no shadow of doubt that they do. Time after time, when I have paused from my work, I have seen one of the does come out into the open and disappear. When the buck appears, he puts his nose down and hunts her line, following every twist and deviation as accurately as a blood hound. The leading doe, followed by her two companions, gradually works her way towards the enclosure where I reared her so that, eventually, all three fetch up at a five-gallon steel drum I have filled with corn for the pheasants. The corn is 'gravity fed', because I have cut narrow slots in the base, just small enough to cause the grains of corn to jam so that they do not trickle to the ground. Pheasants peck at the corn they can see through the slots, which dislodges a few dozen grains which spill out for them to feed on.

But the muntjac have got in on the act. The 'experts' often claim that animals are not intelligent or capable of any form of reason. They only act by instinct. Rubbish! My deer have discovered for themselves that, by bending down and licking up into the slots, they dislodge the corn as efficiently as pheasants with their bills. The prize for following their leader home is to join her at a feast from the corn hopper.

NOTE: *see also* No. 21

19.   Herons' Five-star Menu

We seem to have fewer frogs and toads in our pools than usual, despite a sopping wet spring. Most years, the first sign of winter's end for me is masses of gelatinous eggs, as unappetising as tapioca pudding, floating in the shallow water in two little pools at the edge of the wood. Coupled in torrid embrace are the frogs that laid and fertilised the spawn. Whatever scientists say about such creatures being 'cold blooded', no Latin lover pursues his mate with greater eagerness.

Both frogs and toads spend the winter hibernating from the cold in mud or under stones or roots until they are stirred out of their lethargy by prospects of breeding. The frogs show a leg first and sometimes spawn when there is still ice on the water. Toads are a bit later but often cannot wait until they get to the pool to mate so that the males, which are smaller, hitch a lift by riding piggy-back on the gravid females. The snag is that I am not the only one to notice the arrival of frogs 'that would a-wooing go'.

Our herons are back, too, and it is a load of fisherman's codswallop that herons subsist entirely on fish. They don't. They have a peculiar digestive system which allows them to swallow vast hunks of food whole. I have often watched them stretching and bending their necks as they try to force some apparently unconquerable item of prey to disappear down their insatiable gullets. When they do succeed in sinking the equivalent of an expense account meal, they digest it as easily as any hard-boiled salesman – and eject what they do not need from their bills in neat pellets, like cigar-butts.

There are often dozens of these pellets below the trees where herons roost and nest and the wind soon dries them to the consistency of brittle paper and, by gently teasing them apart, it is easy enough to deduce the precise species of prey the birds have been feeding upon. Naturalists get very skilled at this detective work and it is often possible to amass sufficient evidence to acquit birds like herons of the worst crimes that fishermen lay at their doors. For example, a high proportion of heron pellets is fur and mammal skulls – with neither fish bones nor scales.

The truth is that they will catch almost anything small enough that moves. The remains of water voles and field mice are very commonly found in heron pellets because, while they are standing, statuesque, by the water's edge, voles as well as fish forget they are there.

Perhaps more surprising, the remains of moles also turn up with great regularity. Everyone knows that moles tunnel underground, live largely on earth-worms, and throw up molehills of soil they excavate from their tunnels. So how can birds like herons catch them?

The answer seems to be that, since water finds its own level, the water is usually near the surface of the soil around the edge of pools and streams, so the worms cannot tunnel very deep there and neither can the moles. Indeed, worms frequently come on to the surface to mate in dewy grass at dusk, perhaps for the reason that there is not much room in a wormhole. Moles follow them, feeding on the surface at dusk and dawn, which are favourite times for herons to go fishing – and moles, on the surface, are not as agile as fish in water! So it is easy enough to see why moles and mice so often figure in the pellets that lie beneath the trees of our heronry.

But recently, I have been collecting a few and teasing them out to see if they have changed their menu. I have been disappointed to find the bones of several frogs.

My wife, who is a very keen gardener, is always delighted when I am able to tell her she will be troubled by at least a few less moles this year because the herons are even smarter at catching them than she is. And I don't grudge them as many mice as they can catch because I wage a constant battle in the corn store against the armies of thieves that invade it from the wood. But frogs are different! So many small pools have been filled in to make mechanised farming easier that potential breeding places for frogs and toads get scarcer and scarcer.

Ironically, there are now probably more frogs, toads and newts in pools in suburban gardens than there are in quiet country places.

I dammed up ditches to make our two small pools especially to provide breeding places for them, because there are so many wild duck on the big pool by the house that most of the tadpoles there are eaten even when the adults survive to spawn. So I feel a bit hurt when the herons abuse my hospitality by killing creatures which are equally welcome to share our wildlife reserve!

I have not taken violent action against them, as sportsmen might – but they will not have it so good next year! I am planting the edge of the pool with dense weed so that catching invisible frogs will be harder than hunt-the-slipper!

20.   A Ring Dispels Illusions

A sad little story in a newspaper recently described the plight of a swan pining to death because vandals had shot his mate as she broooded her eggs. Although nobody gets more angry than I do with louts who shoot sitting ducks – or commit other unsporting crimes – I have my doubts about the cause of impending death of the sickly survivor having much to do with a 'broken heart'.

A great many people believe that swans invariably mate for life and that the survivor becomes so distressed when a partner dies that it will go into a decline and fret until it is mercifully released to rejoin its mate in avian immortality. One swan looks pretty much like another swan to

Fishermen's line and litter are the swans' worst enemy

untutored eyes, in the same way that sheep all look the same to everyone but shepherds. The supply of suitable nesting sites rarely matches the demand. So it is a safe bet that swans' nests appear, year after year, near to where there was a nest last year. And since swans are so similar, the assumption is that the pair at a nest one year are the same birds that were there last year. Scientists have shattered such illusions.

Swans happen to be easy birds to catch. They defend their nests and eggs bravely so that bird ringers, armed with long poles with hooks like shepherds' crooks, do not have much difficulty in catching them by the neck and fitting numbered and coloured identification rings to their legs. In July, when the birds are moulting, they drop all the main flight feathers from their wings at once so that they are unable to fly at all for several days. They avoid capture by their natural enemies at this vulnerable stage by settling on lakes and other large sheets of water. They can skulk far from the banks until their new feathers grow and they can seek safety in flight again.

But Nature, which provided them with such an efficient escape mechanism from normal foes, did not take account of the internal combustion engine. Dedicated ornithologists shake off their psychological hang-ups by satisfying their predatory instincts for the pleasures of the chase. They pursue the flightless swans in motor boats, capturing them round the neck with their swan-crooks, whilst convincing themselves that their instinctive excitement has nothing to do with the primitive urge to hunt. The justification is the search for scientific knowledge. And, to prove it, they fit a numbered ring to the leg of every bird they catch before releasing it to swim away unharmed, instead of eating it. Once the rings are fitted, each bird is identified individually as surely as a criminal is forced to leave his fingerprints on police files.

Its circumstances are recorded, and probably stored by computer, so that next time it is caught, there will be no shadow of doubt if it is the same bird that was at the same nest last year or if it simply looks the same. The area where it is caught is also recorded so that, each time it is subsequently caught, the scientists add to their knowledge of how far swans travel, what is the size of their territory, and at what seasons they move from one feeding ground to another. By putting coloured rings as well as numbers on their legs, it is even possible to know where they came from without catching them. But it is the individual numbered

A mute swan makes a splash

rings which unfold the birds' innermost secrets. Records are kept of which bird was paired to which and how many cygnets they reared. And, by numbering the young cygnets, breeding records are compiled over many years to give pedigrees that can be as illustrious as prize-winning cattle or dogs.

Ornithologists have discovered how long the birds live and some of the commonest causes of death. Lead shot, used by fishermen to sink their baited lines, is often picked up and eaten along with natural food. It is ground to powder in the gizzard so that a high proportion of swans die from lead poisoning. Fishermen's lines and other litter left on river banks account for many more.*

There has been a public outcry about the swans from Stratford-upon-Avon, which once vied with William Shakespeare as an attraction for tourists. But now they are almost non-existent there, because of sporting litter-louts and other pollution. Recovery of ornithologists' rings below electric power lines pinpointed the fact that the great birds had fatal collisions with the overhead cables.

But one cause of death that the rings eliminated was the broken heart that the sentimentalists believed was the sequel of the decease of a much-loved mate. There is now hard scientific evidence that, far from mating for life, it is common for a swan to have a new mate next season and not rare to be unfaithful in mid-season. Wife-swapping is by no means the exclusive vice of *homo sapiens*.

* *see Country Wise*, page 76

71

21. Minnie Loses A Leg But Gains A Kid

Some weeks ago, as I was sitting at my desk, casually watching Minnie, the muntjac, feed, I suddenly noticed that she was limping. Examining her more closely through powerful field glasses, I could see that her left back leg was swinging as free as a pendulum. It was quite obviously broken, although the fact that she was feeding suggested that she wasn't in great pain.

So I closed the gap in her enclosure to stop her returning to the wood.

Minnie with her leg in plaster

She is such a tame and trusting little soul that she hopped up on her three good legs and let me pick her up to be examined by the vet. It was far worse than we had thought. The bottom bone of her hind leg was snapped through in two places and a horrid, jagged splinter protruded through the skin. I never discovered how she did it, but it looked as if she had got it fast in a cleft between fallen branches in the wood and panicked to get free.

Although she is full grown, she is no bigger than a fox, so the vet decided to try a very light splint that would not tire her too much while the broken bones were knitting together. The vet straightened the bones, fitted a splint and bound it up as comfortably as possible. I then put her in a darkened shed, with a soft straw bed, to settle down. She gave a few violent kicks and sent the splint and dressing flying.

That was what the vet had feared because the alternatives left were either amputation or putting the whole leg in plaster, over the hock, so that she couldn't dislodge it. The snag in this was that circulation in the lower part of a deer's leg is bad because it is almost entirely skin and bone. She accepted the new treatment without any trouble but, that evening, she was pacing up and down the fence trying to get back into the wood and her mate, Jack, was pacing up and down, trying to get in. It was obviously unsafe to let her out, hampered by a splint, so I let him in, hoping that they would settle together.

Next day I came through the enclosure with the dogs on my way back from the wood: they are perfectly safe with deer and other livestock, and even the wild fallow deer normally ignore them and don't run away. So I was very surprised to see Jack advance, head down and ready to charge, with his bristles up like an angry dog. He left no shadow of doubt that, if the dogs did not go away, he would 'see them off' in no uncertain manner. It made me think because I had seen him mate Minnie some months before and I believed that she would have a kid in the next few weeks. So I crept up to the wooden shelter they often used in very bad weather and peeped in.

Sure enough, there in a corner was a tiny sprite of a kid, no more than a pound or so in weight and half as big as a rabbit. So poor little Minnie had broken her leg one day, had it splinted the next, and kidded – with her leg in plaster – the next. I decided that she would now settle better with the kid than with her mate, so I let Jack return to the freedom of the

A tiny sprite of a kid

wood. I feared that the shock of the broken leg and having it set might prevent her having enough milk to feed the kid. So I watched very closely in case it was necessary to take away the kid and rear it on the bottle.

Two days later, Minnie was pacing the fence again to get out and Jack was equally anxious to get in. It was then I remembered that muntjac deer don't have a normal breeding season but that the doe comes on heat within three days of kidding and is mated right away. That was why they were mad to meet again. The urge to procreate dominated everything else. There was nothing for it but to bow to her wishes, so I let Jack in and he served her, not once but several times, bad leg or not. After that, he lost interest, so I let him out again.

Minnie Loses A Leg But Gains A Kid

After four weeks, the vet returned and we removed the plaster to find the leg had apparently set into perfect shape and seemed as strong as ever. But the next day, it was swinging like a pendulum again, so there was nothing for it but to have another look. The first break had healed perfectly but apparently there had been insufficient blood supply to mend both fractures satisfactorily, so the leg collapsed again. The only thing left was to amputate at the hock.

The vet's deft fingers made a perfect job and, this time, all is well. The stump has healed cleanly and Minnie neither went off her food nor let her milk dry up. The kid is lusty and strong as if its mother had suffered no injury at such a critical time. And Minnie bears us no ill will for the discomfort her treatment must have caused because she returns to the house to feed at night as if nothing untoward had happened.

NOTE: *see also* Nos. 9 and 18

22. Agony In Velvet

An unlikely commodity on the filthy lucre market is the 'velvet' that covers stags' antlers. The velvet covers them for the relatively short time it takes them to grow from tiny buttons on the stag's skull to the spreading antlers beloved by romantic artists. The romance that gives this velvet its astronomic value is the belief, held in some oriental countries, that this covering of the growing antlers of male deer is a powerful aphrodisiac.

The antlers are cast in about May of each year and the stag grows a brand new pair in time for the rutting season in autumn. Immediately after last year's antlers drop off, a tiny button appears on the stag's skull and this growth swells daily as the new antlers develop. While it is growing, the antlers are warm and relatively soft to touch and they are covered with a hairy skin, resembling fine velvet. Beneath are the blood vessels and nerves that feed the growth. At this time, they are extremely tender and sensitive, susceptible to intense irritation by flies and vulnerable to damage if accidentally banged against branches or tough undergrowth. When they are fully developed, the blood supply is sealed off. The antlers grow bony and insensitive and the deer thrashes, or frays off, the velvet to leave a shining pair of new antlers to do battle with rival stags and to impress the does he yearns to mate.

Tired old gentlemen in the Far East imagined that if only they could drink a potion brewed from the velvet that did so much for lovelorn stags, they too would regain the lost virility of youth. So deer farmers in New Zealand discovered that the velvet on growing antlers could be sold for about £150, which was more than the stag's carcase was worth for prime venison. The snag is that collecting it is an exceptionally painful and messy business.

Our Ministry of Agriculture sent a representative to New Zealand to investigate the potential market. The report he issued on his return made horrifying reading. The antlers have to be amputated at such a sensitive stage, that it is necessary to take 'great care' in restraining the deer during and after removal. One method is the injection of a

76

Red stag with just a little bit of velvet left

restraining agent and another is to hold the stag against the wall with leather straps. A local or general anaesthetic may be used and the bleeding staunched by applying a tourniquet, often fashioned from binder twine.

The man from the Ministry added that 'infections are rare and dressings are not normally applied'. He appeared to justify the trade by making the point that, when of good quality, antlers in velvet from one stag can fetch as much as £150. He pointed out that deer farming in New Zealand now concentrates on the production of antlers in velvet rather than venison. 'Antlers in velvet, when sliced or dried,' he reported, 'are used in many traditional oriental medicines.' Which is bureaucratic gobbledegook for aphrodisiacs!

However commercially attractive the proposition may have seemed to him, many of us believe that it is a sordid trade and ethically wrong to inflict such suffering simply to make a quick buck. The Minister of Agriculture immediately asked the Farm Animal Welfare Council to carry out an urgent investigation and to issue a report with their recommendations as quickly as possible.

The Council did not beat about the bush. It stated that, 'There is no overriding need on medical, veterinary or husbandry grounds for amputating antlers in velvet and the economic value should not prevail against the other considerations.' The Council's conclusion was simple and to the point. 'We recommend that the harvesting of antlers in velvet from live deer should be prohibited in Great Britain.' The Minister congratulated them on the speed and thoroughness of their report and promised that the government would act immediately to implement their advice. He added that 'if all the necessary procedures run smoothly,' he hoped that 'the Welfare of Livestock (Deer) Order would be in operation by the time the season for antlers coming into velvet is at its height.'

There are always some who will sink to any depths when there is big money to be made, but the order to prohibit the taking of velvet from live deer was passed in time. Members of the public bombarded their MPs to protest and Parliament – no doubt, with votes in mind – took action to prevent our native deer from being cruelly maltreated in order to jack up the flagging virility of randy Orientals.

23. King Mole Rules The Underworld

My wife and I have a love-hate relationship with moles. I love them – she hates them. She is normally exceptionally soft-hearted and this aggressive quirk in her character is triggered off only when moles destroy some carefully tended treasure in her garden.

I am no gardener. Wild woodland is good enough for me, which may be partly due to the fact that my sort of woodland does not demand nearly as much hard labour as her garden does. The other evening we were sitting on the lawn, relaxing after a perfect day, when she went rigid in her seat. 'Do you see what I see?' she asked. I did.

On the bed by the edge of the lawn, she had planted out some flowers she had cossetted with loving care all winter. Her one mistake had been to lavish them with well-rotted farmyard manure, which would have made any muck-and-magic health food farmer drool with envy. In addition to growing health-giving food, which the devotees imagine gives them eternal youth, honest farmyard muck encourages the earthworms.

Earthworms encourage moles, so the king mole of the district decided, unwisely at it turned out, to tunnel immediately under my wife's pride and joy, the idea being that the worms which were attracted by the farmyard muck would tumble into his tunnel, so that all he would have to do would be to scuttle along beneath them and scoff them up. Unluckily for him, he chose the wrong time to set his tunnel trap.

The sight that had made Jess wonder if the evidence of her eyes was to be believed was a large bunch of gorgeous flowers rocking about as if a hurricane had hit them. I confirmed the awful truth. The cause of the commotion was the mole, tunnelling just below the surface and making a cavern under the roots, which would dry them out and wither the plants.

One of my few party tricks, guaranteed to astonish all beholders, is to creep up to where a mole can be seen raising the surface soil, and to leap into the air, landing with a foot each side of where the mole is digging his tunnel. When all goes well, the poor fellow is so terrified at having his tunnel blocked behind him with one heavy foot, with the other foot a few inches in front of his nose, that he pops out on to the surface like a cork out of a bottle.

Determined to capture the mole that was wreaking havoc in the garden, I went into action with my well-rehearsed routine. My quarry did not co-operate, but shot either sideways or downwards to escape. All that happened was that my big feet crushed the plants he hadn't dug out, and he got the fright of his life.

There are, of course, other ways of dealing with moles in gardens, though my experience is that none of them is very effective. It is far easier to avoid gardening, as I do, but some fanatics with spade and fork put thorny rose briars down the tunnels under the delusion that the raiders will be deterred by the prickles. All that usually happens is that it is the gardener who packs up first as the moles make new tunnels.

Some try mothballs, or the expensive stuff advertised in glossy magazines; Ministry rat-catchers use worms poisoned with strychnine. The only effective method that I know was the old-fashioned mole-catcher, who trapped them and sold their pelts for waistcoats. As such glamorous gear has fallen out of fashion, the few surviving mole-catchers have joined the exalted ranks of pest officers who use scientific gimmicks that never seem to work.

Whatever the gardeners think of moles, I confess to a deep affection for them, especially in their rightful place in woodland. The soil there is never turned over because nobody could dig or plough through the roots. So, left to itself, it would simply be composed of year after year's layer of leaves, left to rot eventually into peat. Worms and spiders and insects live here and the moles earn their living making tunnels under the surface. Their prey falls into the tunnel so that it is lying ready to be eaten next time the tunneller makes the round of his territory. When it rains, the tunnels act as Nature's drains and moles, constantly turning over the soil, produce as fine a tilth of rich humus as gardeners could make in their compost heaps. The mole hills that erupt on the surface form the perfect seed bed for acorns and the seeds of other plants and trees.

So whatever harm the moles may do in my wife's garden, 'my' moles do me nothing but good in the wood, where they create a great variety of fertility. The mere thought of the energy they must expend in driving their tunnels through virgin soil makes me sink back in my deck chair with exhaustion and reach for a drink. So my advice to local moles is to enjoy the hospitality of the wood and keep out of the garden. My party trick may work better next time!

24. Barn Owls In Danger

In some parts of the country, the scientists blame the decline in the population of barn owls on the felling of dead elms. They say that elm trees have exactly the type of hollows that barn owls choose to make their nests and that, if they are deprived of the desirable sites they need, they simply do not breed. There is no shadow of doubt that barn owls have become relatively rare birds since I was young. But I doubt if much of the blame can be fairly laid at the door of the declining elms.

Fifty years ago, most tall brick-built barns had a platform, high in the rafters of the roof, with holes left in the gable ends exactly like a dove cote. It wasn't messy pigeons the farmers sought to attract. Corn was stored in sacks, in those days, and rats and mice were a plague that not only consumed large quantities of grain but also wrought havoc by gnawing holes in sacks, allowing the grain to spill out. So every farm had its complement of half-fed cats, who were expected to make up their diet with succulent young rats and mice.

The law laid down that, when ricks were threshed, they must be surrounded by small mesh wire netting so that any rats lurking there could be caught by dogs or clobbered with sticks when the last sheaves of corn were pitched out. Farmers also knew that the best cats and dogs will not kill all the rats and mice where tons of corn are stored in often inaccessible places. They knew that barn owls are nature's natural control so the platforms they erected in their rafters were designed for owls not pigeons.

Success was widespread and obvious. As a lad, I could have gone to half a dozen barns within a couple of miles of my home in Bloxwich and heard the characteristic 'snoring' noise which young owls make while waiting to be fed on summer nights, and seen the ghost-like white shadows of parents on their silent wings. The real decline came after the war, and I believe that part of the cause was the change in farming methods. Combine harvesters were all the rage and corn was harvested and stored in bulk, so that there were less sacks of corn to provide perfect sanctuary for rats and mice. Government rat-catchers also

The barn owl is amongst our most beautiful birds

changed their methods. Instead of turning up on a bicycle, with a bag of ferrets and a few terriers, they rode up in vans with poison in the back. They undoubtedly exterminated a lot of the rats and mice – but they didn't all die suddenly. Predators, including owls, that caught them after they had eaten the poison, naturally suffered from secondary poisoning.

This was aggravated by prey they caught in the fields. Chemical pesticides used to protect crops affect a wide range of wildlife as well as the pests they are designed to exterminate. Owls catching these before they have died are equally vulnerable. Colour is lent to this theory by the fact that barn owls have suffered more than tawny owls, which feed largely in woodlands untouched by agricultural sprays and other poisons. Barn owls have also suffered more in arable areas than they have in dairying areas, where less chemicals are used.

Barn Owls In Danger

Some years ago, I had a delightful barn owl called Fred.* He had been hatched in a traditional owl cote in a barn not far away, but tumbled out before he could fly and was reared by the farmer's family. When he started to fly round the farmyard, the other owls had forgotten him and chivvied him off like a stranger, so the farmer asked me to take him. He was so dependent on humans finding his food that it took months before he had learned to catch prey for himself, by which time we had grown so fond of him that parting was a real wrench. He stayed around for six weeks or so, settling in an owl cote I had built for him in the outbuilding. Then he moved down to the village and roosted in a pear tree at the doctor's house.

For a while he still came back to my feeding point for mice and sliced pigeon which I left out, but as he gradually grew more self-reliant he came less often. We haven't seen him now for years, but we hope he travelled a little further over to Blithfield reservoir to join barn owls that still hunt along the banks there.

Owls are surprisingly easy to breed in captivity and some naturalists are regularly breeding and liberating several each year and establishing them, mainly in isolated barns, in wild hill country. There they are less in danger from catching and eating the victims of poisonous pesticides so widely used on arable farms. They are among our most beautiful birds and they do nothing but good to mankind. The least we can do is to provide a safe enough environment for them to survive.

* *see Country Seasons*, pages 53 and 65

25. The Guest Who Played Host

We spent most of our holiday with our heads in the clouds. Not, I hasten to add, because we were particularly delighted but because when it rains in Wales every road is lost in mist at the top of every minor mountain. And it rained on every one of the three days we were away.

Fellow holiday makers were stuffed with gloom and moaned incessantly about the miserable Welsh weather, but we had gone properly equipped and felt smugly superior. It was a sentimental journey to revisit old haunts. I hate holidays and would never go away except to give my wife a break from housework.

If I could choose my ideal holiday, regardless of expense, I would hire a butler and a cook for a week at home, live like a lord without doing a tap, and ask my friends for endless parties. That is impossible unless I win the pools, which is unlikely since I don't fill in the form, so we settled for the next best thing.

About thirty years ago, we discovered a hotel in central Wales that came close to our ideal. One of its chief attractions was that so few people went there, so wild horses wouldn't drag from me precisely where it is in case we want to go there again. Hearing that it had recently come under new management, we decided to call to see if the standards had slipped. Although it is quite a large hotel, with twenty-seven bedrooms and two lounges, there never seemed to be more than a dozen guests when we first went there. The reason was interesting. The proprietor rarely put in an appearance and the place was virtually run by one of the guests who lived there permanently.

He was a perfectly delightful Canadian major who had been terribly burned when he had been shot from an aeroplane in the First World War. The injury was so extensive that he couldn't stand the winter in his native land: when he was invalided out of the Air Force, he had come to 'our' hotel to recuperate, and stayed to make it his permanent home.

The setting is superb. A tumbling river through the grounds supplies fishing for trout and salmon. When the river isn't in the right mood to disgorge its fish, there is a lake as an alternative: dippers nest under the waterfall that feeds the lake. The grounds wind away through a steeply-wooded valley where buzzards and pied flycatchers nest, and there were even red squirrels when we first found it.

Since the proprietor didn't seem very interested in making a fortune, there was real danger that the place might fold up, so the major ran the bar and the fishing. All that was necessary for him to continue living in this paradise was that there should be just enough profit to keep things ticking over, so he picked and chose the guests. If he didn't like them, the service in the bar would leave much to be desired, to put it mildly, and the chances of getting a fishing beat with any fish were minimal. Outsiders went off in high dudgeon. If the major liked you, on the other hand, all was sweetness and light and the chances were that you would like the other guests as well because they, too, were hand-picked, against the same yardstick.

What puzzled us was why the proprietor had ever got entangled so far from the city lights. He was an extremely dapper little man, obviously well-educated and cultured. His suave manners and pin-stripe suit seemed strangely out of place in an obscure fishing hotel in central Wales. The explanation was fascinating – if improbable. Rumour had it that the proprietor had been an up-and-coming city banker who had got the whisper that an enormous reservoir was to be built in Wales to feed Birmingham. There was a financial killing for anyone who could make a scoop by buying up land before the developers got it. And the budding tycoon convinced his partners that he was the key to their fortune.

So he was sent to wildest Wales to buy up land, and his silver tongue worked miracles. The last key place to be flooded was to be 'our' hotel. He bought it and went back to London in triumph to celebrate – only to receive a nasty shock. Plans had changed and Birmingham was to get water from elsewhere. Our tycoon had purchased the wrong valley! Not unnaturally, his banker friends were furious. As punishment, they banished their partner to the back-of-beyond he had bought by mistake.

It made a good story because the appearance of the debonair

proprietor lent it so much colour that it just could be true. But I never believed it – until our recent holiday. Hanging in the hall was an old ordnance map with plans for a reservoir hatched in. 'Our' hotel was certainly once scheduled to be flooded at the tail of the reservoir. If it had been, we should have missed some of the best holidays of our lives – and the proprietor might have died a millionaire!

26. Winged Wonders

Our horse-stingers have been out in force this week, but they haven't stung a horse. It's pretty ignorant to call them horse-stingers, if only because they haven't got a sting. Some country folk call them the devil's darning needles, due to their long tapering bodies, horse adders or snake doctors. Boffins call them *Odonata* but to me, and I expect to you, they are simply dragonflies.

The little pool down the wood is fringed with bushes with a medley of reeds and rushes at the edge. Growing in the depths are swathes of water weed. When the sun comes out in August, so do our dragonflies. Part of my bank holiday this year was spent far from chattering crowds, watching the dragonflies hunting along the woodland rides and along the water edge.

Horses might *think* that insects with three-inch bodies, with four gauzy wings to match, are dangerous because they do *look* as if they could sting. And I was certainly brought up to believe they could. There is no more truth in the belief than the one that says newts, or askers, can spit fire. But smaller insects have every reason to regard them as dragons because they are mighty hunters, equipped with weapons of attack that give their prey very little chance of a fair run for their money.

They have enormous eyes. These stick out of each side of their head, bulbous as a space man's goggles, and each eye has a mosaic of about thirty thousand facets, facing up, down, forwards and back. They provide vision in every direction at once without so much as a flick of the head. And, although they look as beautiful as craftsman-cut diamonds to me, they must seem as sinister as enemy radar to their potential victims. Not only can they see all round, but they can follow the fastest movement more than five times as easily as we can. A sprinter whose feet put our vision in a blur would appear as a pathetic slow motion to a dragonfly. It isn't much good being equipped to see your quarry if you can't catch it, but these magnificent insects score there, too. Their four wings propel streamlined bodies whose aerodynamic perfection leaves the brightest boffins in aircraft design offices wheezing at the starting post.

They can fly faster than other insects – and most birds. They can twist and turn in pursuit and even fly backwards. No wonder another name for them is darters! There are over forty different species of dragonfly in this country and over five thousand species spread over the whole world. In prehistoric times, one great brute had a wing span of over four feet – and I reckon that one would have made most folk run for cover. But our pool also sports a few flamboyant damsel flies, with iridescent colours as brilliant as kingfishers, but with folding wings and only about half the size of the horse-stingers that attract me so much. These are the chaps which fascinate me and recently I shared the thrills of the chase with them.

In August, the tree tops literally hum with flies, some of which zoom in to sup on whoever is bold enough to venture into their territory. So

The dragonfly – a masterpiece of creation

it's encouraging to see such biters bit. Three or four dragonflies were patrolling their territory as regularly as fighter planes waiting for an enemy raid. Occasionally, one would peel off to give chase to a succulent fly which didn't really have a chance. Duck and weave as it would, the hunter overtook it and clasped it in his feet, carrying it off looking like a tiny bomb strapped to the undercarriage of a plane. There was no quarter. The dragonfly nipped off its victims wings and head and sucked the body as dry as a husk. Then, off again on the next patrol.

They don't stand any nonsense among themselves either. If a stranger comes on their territory, they see him off without ceremony. But young dragonflies are worse. They hatch from eggs into miniature insects which live for up to five years under water before emerging on to a reed, shedding their skin and changing into an adult insect, as a butterfly hatches from a chrysalis. Under water, of course, they don't need wings so that, in a way, they look far more like conventional dragons than the adults do, with large heads equipped with devastating pincer jaws, and stockier bodies. They creep around the murky depths, as sinister as submarines, pouncing on any living creature that crosses their path. They clasp any soft part of their victim with hollow jaws, through which they suck the vital juices before their quarry has time to die with dignity.

I have seen them eat huge tadpoles, young newts and sizeable fish. But a favourite item on their menu is other dragonfly larvae, and what prevents them proliferating into a plague is the fact that they are cannibals and feed upon each other! Theirs is a harsh world where only the fittest survive but such ruthless natural selection results in a crop of huge insects in our wood which are not only supremely beautiful but useful too because they prey on the flies that would otherwise have preyed on me.

27. Garden Blitz Leaves Orphan In Trouble

Recently, someone telephoned me to say that she was caring for a baby hedgehog but was unable to persuade it to feed. She said that its prickles had not yet stiffened from silky hairs to hard spines and that its eyes were not yet open, from which I could deduce that it could be no more than a few days old. It had been found 'abandoned' in her neighbour's garden, which immediately aroused my suspicions. Wild creatures are not normally abandoned by their parents and the usual explanation is that the mother has been disturbed while moving or feeding her young, and has thought that discretion was the better part of valour, so has retreated till the coast is clear.

This happens most often with fledgling birds which have just scattered from the nest and are screaming to be fed. If they are left to themselves, the old birds will soon hear them and come along to feed them. 'Rescuing' them is not the kindness it may seem!

So I made a few pointed enquiries and discovered that the woman's neighbour had just moved in to find an overgrown and dilapidated garden, just the sort of habitat that would provide a growing family of hedgehogs with the insects and cover that they would consider five-star luxury. However, the new owners of the garden did not see it that way. They mounted a blitz and slimmed down the undergrowth to convert the chaos into order.

The disturbance did not suit the hedgehogs, whose ideas of peace and quiet did not include human monsters wielding garden forks and spades. The gardeners were alerted when they suddenly noticed a hedgehog waddling across the lawn with something in her mouth. They saw that she was carrying a baby hedgehog and that there were three more, lying on the ground beside the compost heap, which was by now in the process of being spread about the flower beds.

They waited quietly and the mother returned twice to collect the youngsters, which had been accidently forked out of their nest. But she didn't come for the fourth. It was impossible to decide if this was because she became suspicious of the intruders or if it was simply because she couldn't count.

So it was decided to leave the tiny creature where it was in the hope that its mother would screw up her courage, when things quietened down, and reunite him with his brothers. It didn't work out like that. Next morning he was still lying on his back, stiff, cold and apparently lifeless. He was picked up and taken to the neighbour who telephoned me. She is known to have a soft heart and winning ways with animals and for this reason she asked me not to divulge her name, because she could not cope with the deluge of waifs and strays that arrive on such kind people's doorsteps. Although she has dealt with lots of fledgling birds, this was the first time a hedgehog had landed in her lap, which was precisely where it was when she telephoned me.

The warmth of her hands had kindled a spark of life but, try as she might, she hadn't been able to tempt it to feed. This was partly because she had offered it cow's milk, which is too strong for such a small creature, and partly because she hadn't warmed the milk. I told her to buy a doll's bottle from a toy shop and make a hole in the teat, which is usually 'blind'. Failing this a piece of ordinary valve rubber, sold for bicycle tyres, is quite good when attached to an eye dropper. The most suitable food is ordinary baby food made from dried milk powder, or the special food sold by pet shops for rearing puppies. I added that it might be necessary to force feed for a day or two, until he developed a taste for artificial baby food – and I know from experience how difficult it is to force feed such tiny creatures.

I know plenty of people who have reared hedgehogs from tiny piglets and they have always turned out perfectly delightful. They become tame and confiding and will sometimes settle down and adopt the garden of their owner as their lifelong home.

However, I foresee a snag if this hedgehog is reared successfully. The middle of September is quite late enough for hedgehogs to be born, even if they can grow up under perfect, natural conditions. Hedgehogs hibernate in winter and, before they fall asleep, they must have put on enough fat to last them through until spring. This fat acts as an eiderdown to keep them warm, but they also absorb it to take the place of normal food.

A rule-of-thumb is that if a hedgehog does not weigh a pound when he hibernates, he will not survive to see the spring. The alternative might be, in this case, to prevent him hibernating by the simple expedient of keeping him in a warm room throughout the winter because it is the dropping temperature which sets off hibernation. Even if he is carefully fed, watered and kept warm throughout the winter, the odds against him are tremendous; yet what a feather in her cap if his rescuer succeeds!

28. The Farmers' Dilemma

A neighbouring farmer on his routine evening rounds to check his livestock spotted a stranger crossing the field where the 'bachelor' rams were paddocked. Their bachelorhood is but temporary because next month, October, they will be introduced to the fair pastures to mate their ewes and produce next year's crop of lambs. Although the sheep in TV ads seem like woolly, cuddly toys, real rams, fretting to get on with their destined job, can be truculent and aggressive.

So my neighbour leaned over the gate to watch the fun. Sure enough, the senior sheep took exception to the uninvited guest, lowered his head and charged. His unsuspecting target strode on in blissful ignorance until what must have felt like a sledge hammer struck him in the seat of his pants and launched him into orbit. My neighbour gathered from his remarks that he is likely to take his breakfast standing up in the near future, and when he recovers he intends to seek fresh pastures to explore. He was very cross indeed.

He was also fairly lucky to have got away with the encounter comparatively unscathed. A hundredweight of mutton-on-the-hoof takes a bit of stopping at thirty miles an hour, and a ram's skull is as hard as the battering-ram that was named after his distant ancestor. It can quite easily break a strong man's thigh.

In spite of this, nobody in his senses would expect farmers to keep sheep out of their fields. It is an integral part of their living. Yet attitudes to bulls are very different. Cows come in season once in three weeks and remain receptive to the bull for only twenty-four hours. There is no obvious sign when the females are in the mood for love and it needs a skilled cowman in the close quarters of a milking parlour to gauge precisely when introductions are in order. It is virtually impossible to tell this when beasts are roaming free in the field, except, of course, for a bull. So for centuries past, sensible farmers have run a bull loose with their herds of cows in the certain knowledge that the lucky chap would lose no time in getting his mates in calf at the earliest possible moment. Failure to do so would result in the loss of three weeks before the next generation of calves were born, which is three weeks longer than necessary between each crop of calves, during which the mother would consume another three weeks' ration of food.

All countrymen know this and, when I was young, all countrymen expected to find bulls in any field where there were cows when they went out in the countryside. Sensible countrymen also know that no bull is to be trusted, so they give all bulls a wide berth. Some bulls, of course, are worse than others and it is usual for breeds that have been selectively bred to produce milk, such as Fresians, to be more unpredictable and dangerous than breeds like white-faced Herefords, which look more massive and masculine. Worst of all are the pretty little Jerseys and Guernseys.

So there is a great deal of wheeling and dealing going on behind the scenes to influence the contents of the forthcoming Wildlife and

Companions on your walk: cattle on the Pennine Way near Skipton in Yorkshire

Countryside Bill. Farmers, who have to wrest a living from the land, not unnaturally want the right to put their bulls wherever it is reasonable to graze cows. Ramblers and others who are jealous of the rights to use footpaths unhampered, claim that no bull should be turned out in any field crossed by a public footpath.

It is partly a question of priorities. Farmers regard their land as a factory to produce food as cheaply and efficiently as possible. Visitors from towns tend to regard the green fields as their playground. It looks, at the moment, as if we are due for a typically British compromise. The Department of the Environment is suggesting that 'beef' bulls, reputed to be safer, should be allowed in fields with footpaths provided they are accompanied by mature cows or heifers to maintain their concentration. 'Dairy' breeds, on the other hand, would be forced to confine their courtship to fields where it would be trespass to wander.

Once the principle is established that *no* bulls can be turned out in fields where the public can wander, it would be logical to exclude stallions as well. They can be equally dangerous. Where 'rights' are concerned, reason too often flies out the window.

I can see both sides and some farmers, whose land is criss-crossed by footpaths, are certainly more affected than others. The reasonable compromise seems to me to be to rationalise footpaths to meet modern conditions. They were originally made when fields were small, not for strangers' leisure but for the convenience of employees and neighbours to get to work or school.

Fields are now larger to cope with modern mechanisation and it might be possible to have far fewer footpaths, but to site them to include the best views and variety of countryside while doing the minimum damage to productive farming operations.

NOTE: The Wildlife and Countryside Bill succeeded in annoying both sides by making it illegal to put *dairy* bulls in fields with footpaths but legal for *beef* bulls. Ignorant visitors say they can't tell a beef bull from a dairy bull, so they are cross. Farmers are cross because the cost of artificial insemination is rising and they want to put dairy bulls with cattle as well as beef bulls.

29.   Gateway To The Wild

A chap recently sent me a sad little note asking why it was that, on a holiday in the Forest of Dean, he and his wife saw few signs of wildlife. 'Birds were scarce,' he said. 'All I found was one set of deer tracks. As you know, if there is anyone human around, they're off.'

Yes, I do know – but I don't believe that 'there was nothing much but wandering sheep' in the Forest of Dean. All that happened was that he didn't see it. I spent a great deal of time watching birds and animals wherever I go, and it is fair to say that I see less while I am walking than when I have time to stand and wait.

When I see gaggles of hikers, kitted out like pantomime explorers in clumpy boots, flamboyant anoraks and woolly hats, I am not surprised that they see little but the scenery. You can hear them chattering a quarter of a mile before they arrive. Garments that were designed to be spotted miles away by mountain rescue squads are obtrusive to everything else and a mass of sweaty humanity gives adequate warning of its approach to any wild creatures downwind.

To get clued up about how to see what's what, watch a professional gamekeeper. His clothes are ancient and weatherbeaten so that mud-stained macs and battered hats merge with autumn-tinted leaves. He is usually a taciturn man so that, if he doesn't walk alone, his monosyllabic grunts to his sole companion make even less noise than his feet, which scarcely crack a twig. Yet even he will see less while on the move than when he is standing still. I often have mentioned that I am a confirmed leaner-on-gates. So are most gamekeepers.

Gateways, because they are at the junction of two fields or between woodland and fields, usually command a view of stretches of land along the boundaries between arable and pasture or farmland and woods. That is just the type of land that wild creatures have to cross to leave their beds for feeding or their feeding grounds to lie up. Anyone who stays still against a gateway for long enough appears to melt into the woodwork until he becomes part of it. While he is still, he is almost invisible. Birds and animals which heard or saw him approach prob-

I always make time to stand and wait and watch

ably have made themselves scarce and disappeared, but it isn't long before they peep out to see if the coast is clear. Because the intruder has merged with his surroundings, his arrival will be forgotten and he will have a front row in the stalls to watch whatever drama unfolds.

Gamekeepers use the ploy to destroy their foes and, when the hated fox or crow emerges, the crack of a rifle is the final curtain to a one-act play.

Harmless onlookers, on the other hand, can enjoy tender love scenes as hares perform their wild courtship dances, or they can hear the lilting songs of shy birds at close quarters, or watch the blood-and-thunder tragedies as a predator captures his prey.

Some gates, of course, are better vantage points than others, so that it is an enormous advantage to be a bit of a detective. Footprints in the mud of well-worn tracks are rich in clues. The slots of cloven-hooved deer or badger tracks, with their five toes, are more reliable evidence of a star quality than any critic of the human stage.

Yet it is also vital to know the time of the performance. Matinees are usually poorly attended in wild places, not so much by the audience as by the performers. Deer, foxes and badgers are at their best at dawn and dusk. So perhaps my correspondents went out in the Forest of Dean when the creatures they wanted to see were in bed. I certainly see more when I am perched on a vantage point before breakfast or after supper than in the rest of the day put together.

Birds, of course, are easier to spot than animals except, perhaps, in the months of July and August, while they are moulting. They are then so sore and miserable that they skulk out of sight. But in spring, their song gives them away and all that is necessary is to settle comfortably where the melody is loudest. They soon will give away the site they have chosen to nest by carrying material or feeding their mates or young.

The best way to watch birds in winter is to locate their feeding grounds or where they roost and to settle motionless to watch. Bird-watchers throng the banks of every reservoir and river because ducks and wildfowl concentrate there in greatest numbers, so it needs no skill to find them. The very fact that any mug can see them there destroys the attraction for me, because I prefer the reward of using my skill to watch them.

30. Legacy Of Hunting Kings

Most people think of lawns as the shaven patches of velvety turf that form the perfect backcloth to gorgeous flower gardens. Lawn can also spell boredom, when mowing it, or convivial evenings with fellow sufferers in the local, replacing lost sweat by pints of honest ale, as a reward for such a sentence of hard labour. Lawns were nothing like that in the good old days. They were simply clearings in a forest.

Long before William the Conqueror arrived in 1066, King Canute, famous for failing to keep dry feet when the tide was coming in, had done better in the hunting field. He had rather a one-track mind and he was so fond of hunting that he had chucked out the native inhabitants from huge tracts of potentially good hunting country to make Royal Forests where only the King and his pals could enjoy the pleasures of the chase. Penalties for poaching were pretty tough. Canute laid down that every Freeman could have the game and vert on his own territory, but without the right of the chase. 'And let all abstain from mine,' he added, 'wherever I wish to have it.'

He made certain there was no misunderstanding by imposing a fine of twice the value for the first two convictions for poaching, 'while he who offended thrice forfeited all he was worth to the King'. Anyone who was caught killing a Royal Beast (which was a stag the king himself used to hunt) could lose his freedom or his life, depending on his social status!

But it wasn't as simple as that. Every gamekeeper knows you don't create a good shoot simply by controlling the poachers. Before it is a good shoot, you have got to have something to shoot.

To achieve this, modern keepers make certain that the cover is attractive, that it shelters the game, and that there is plenty of food to feed it. To provide these conditions in a forest, it was vital to have clearings, to grow herbage, as well as thickets in which the deer could lie up. These clearings were called lawns. Maps of any ancient forests mark these lawns clearly and, on the map of our wood, which was once part of the ancient forest of Needwood, the clearing at the end is marked

Daffodil Lawn. Across the drive, on my neighbour's farm, one field is marked Great Lawn, though it is now indistinguishable from acres of others because the whole of his farm has been 'reclaimed' for agriculture.

Clearings in wild forests don't stay clear unless you do something about them. They revert to wild scrubland. So our forefathers were allowed by the King to turn cattle and pigs and horses into the forest, to feed and to cut logs to burn on their hearths. They were allowed to cut bracken for litter for their stock to lie on – but let no man poach the game, not only of the King but of any of his betters! The Bishop of Lichfield, for example, had the hunting rights over 110,000 acres in the Midlands, including Cannock Chase. Such sporting parsons, alas, are now a thing of the past. While they lasted, their sporting estates were kept in good order by the local inhabitants' desire to keep the lawns as productive as possible for their own cattle. What the deer ate was, in effect, the rent they paid.

Times have changed since then. Such labour-intensive tasks as cutting bracken by hand for bedding is now uneconomic. Forest drains, which were cut and maintained as winter jobs when there was nothing much else to do, have fallen into disrepair. One of the worst affected areas is the New Forest, which was once one of the favourite hunting grounds of William the Conqueror (or William the Bastard, as poachers dubbed him). Lawns in the New Forest have got snarled up with hawthorn and bramble scrubs, the drains have got blocked, making boggy land where there used to be good grazing, and bracken is invading the clearings.

So the Forestry Commission has got the go-ahead to restore some of the more famous lawns before it is too late. Jerry Wiggin, of the Ministry of Agriculture, jumped on the bandwagon to co-ordinate the exercise. He wrote to the chairman of the Forestry Commission, telling him that 'treatment will need to be seen to be sympathetic', which is like teaching his grandmother to suck eggs, as the Forestry Commission has a far better track record for handling wildlife problems than has the Ministry of Agriculture. But the fact that Mr Wiggin considered it necessary to labour the point, and to say that Ministry of Agriculture engineers 'will see that the Water Authorities do not unnecessarily deepen the river bed or create canal-like courses which would look unsightly', is some measure of public concern.

The fact is that there are tremendous differences of opinion between conservationists, hikers, sportsmen and ordinary countryfolk about what should take priority. In a number of the lawns in question, for example, the scrub that has grown up in some of the boggy patches is favourable for dragonflies. The Nature Conservancy Council naturally tries to further the interests of wildlife – and the votes that naturalists cast. So they are concerned about the destruction of habitat that is vital for the insects they cherish. The fact that the scrub has only grown up because the original terrain was neglected passes over their heads.

Folk who escape to the Forest for its peace and beauty love the gorgeous autumn colours of, among other things, bracken as it runs the gamut of tints from brilliant green to gold. They are glad that the commoners no longer find it economic to harvest the bracken for bedding. The fact that it crowds out productive keep for stock means less to them.

There will always be conflicts between those who wish to use the countryside as a factory to produce food and those who regard it as the perfect place for leisure – between sportsmen, naturalists and farmers. So it is heartening to find that the Forestry Commission and Ministries of Agriculture and of the Environment can get together to preserve our heritage in the New Forest.

31. The Fox That Lost Its Head

A woman from Birmingham asked me to solve a mystery that made the horror stories of fiction seem flabby by comparison. It concerned the case of a mutilated fox. The crime was discovered in a Birmingham garden when the woman saw the body of a fox on her lawn.

'On looking closer,' she continued, 'I found the head had been completely severed from the body. Very cleanly done. The tail was about five feet away from the body. I looked everywhere for traces of the head, but could not find anything.'

Her husband said that he would bury the body, but as time was short, he wrapped it tidily in a dustbin-liner and left it until the evening. It was put by the compost heap at the bottom of the garden but, as it rained that evening, the body was left in the plastic bag. The story did not end there. . . . Next morning, the plastic bag was blowing around the garden – empty!

'There was absolutely no sign of the fox. It had just disappeared, leaving not a bone or whisker.'

She asked if foxes eat each other, describing the victim as not very bright in colour, but well-rounded and plump, and added that, as far as she could make out, the animal was a vixen. The scene of the crime was within three miles of the city centre. And since the garden is enclosed by hedges and tall trees, nobody could possibly have thrown the body over the fence – or placed the tail neatly a few feet from the body, if they had. Nor, I imagine, could a human culprit have climbed over the hedge to remove the remains from the plastic bag by the compost heap the next night.

A detailed examination of the body showed that the head had been 'very tidily' chewed off. The final clue was that none of the neighbours kept dogs and the household dog was the only one with access to the garden – and he was 'very timid'. So he can be discounted. Foxhounds will eat a fox, in the heat of the moment, when their blood is up, at the

An urban fox finds his breakfast . . . with no trouble at all

end of a long and successful hunt. 'Breaking him up', the huntsmen call it. But no ordinary dog of my acquaintance shows the least interest in *dead* foxes. Apart, perhaps, from rolling on them as they will roll on a number of powerfully scented objects, particularly carrion when it is going 'high'. Even foxhounds spurn stale fox.

The next clue was the colour. 'Not very bright' was the description. Fox cubs have woolly coats when they are young, and they do not acquire the sophisticated sleekness beloved by slinky blondes until they moult into adult coats. So the body was a young female, because my informant said that it appeared to be a vixen.

She also said that 'foxes gain access to the garden by jumping a six-foot slatted fence beyond the hedge, or through a small hole, on the other side into a neighbour's garden.' A well-grown cub would have been too heavy for the strongest dog fox to carry in his jaws as he leaped over a six-foot fence, and the difficulties of pulling the victim through a 'small' hole in the other fence are obvious. So it seemed possible the fox actually died in the garden, either because it was attacked there, or because it was already ill or injured, and crawled there to die.

My own guess – and it was no more than a guess – was that the cub was dying when it arrived, probably from an accident, such as being hit by a car. The more interesting question was – what decapitated it and subsequently removed the body? I had very little doubt that this was another fox, because foxes are among the few animals that will eat the flesh of fox, which is foul-smelling and rank of flavour. Carrion crows and magpies would also eat it, but would not be strong enough to chew off the head 'tidily'.

In support of my theory, I happen to have carried out experiments myself some years ago. Foxes are by far the most dangerous carriers of rabies. And when rabies comes to this country, as it surely will unless we tighten controls on smuggling animals from the continent, the Ministry of Agriculture proposes to poison foxes for miles around the outbreak. The poison they initially proposed was strychnine, and the bait they would dope would be the heads of poultry. I happen to think that this would be grossly irresponsible because many creatures besides foxes would eat chicken heads (dogs and cats, for example) and because strychnine is so persistent. My experiment was designed to find a less dangerous alternative.

Gamekeeepers have often told me that foxes regard gamey fox as a delicacy, and that they will also eat dead rat, which is spurned by most other animals. These are the baits keepers use when foxes are raiding their pheasants and they want to be sure not to poison the boss's dog by mistake. To test their claim, I have shot several foxes in my wood and left them to see what happened. My experience has been that, when they acquire the right degree of ripeness, something devours them. I refuse to use poison of any sort in my wood, but keeper friends assure me that if I did, the culprit I should find would be a fox that had dined too well – but not wisely.

My guess is that the decapitated fox had died by accident or natural causes and added to the menu of other scavaging urban foxes.

32. Spin Another Yarn

My father, who was a family doctor, stood no messing from malingering patients. A common ailment, real and imagined, in his mining practice was 'bad back'. Some of his patients' bad backs were all too genuine, caused by working in the constricted spaces of underground coal seams. Others were just an excuse for a few days 'on the box'.

His diagnostic thumb probed ruthlessly, producing howls of agony from seekers of time-off at taxpayers' expense, because he knew spots so sensitive that the patient would never return unless he really had to. Genuine chaps, who really had hurt themselves, were instantly eased by his gentle physiotherapy and were fixed up with a relaxing period to recover.

The first time he called at a new patient's house, his sharp eyes probed every cranny for signs of a spider's web. If he couldn't find one, he reckoned he was in for a good deal of trouble because housewives that are so prissy that they never give a spider a chance to spin her web are just the sort of house-proud hypochondriacs who would call him out for every snivelling cold or petty finger-ache. He had a far greater respect for spiders than for such spit-and-polishers.

Spiders' webs, he informed me, were ideal for staunching wounds provided, of course, that they were nice, clean, country spiders' webs and not coated in layers of city murk and dust. They were good for staunching wounds because their threads were so fine that the fluffiest cotton wool could not equal them for spreading the blood from the wound so that it came in contact with the maximum area of air to oxydise it and cause it to clot.

There was another major advantage. Spiders' webs carried electro-static charges which actually repelled similar charged bacteria, which might otherwise have caused infection. So a wound covered by a spider's web not only stopped bleeding more quickly than if it had been dressed by more conventional dressings, but it was less likely to go wrong.

The irony was that, although my father let me into such mysteries, he didn't actually practise what he preached because it would have been frowned upon by conventional doctors – who are usually so hidebound about using folk medicine that does not appear in the syllabus of the teaching hospital.

Knowledge about the static electrical charge of cobwebs has only come to light since my father died and it has also been discovered that silk glands, where the web is spun, were evolved from the poison glands of primitive hunting spiders. This poison promotes blood clotting in the victim and people who die after being bitten by a Black Widow spider get coronary thrombosis and massive blood clotting.

So my old man wasn't so far wrong. He was right about the effect though he didn't know the cause. Spiders' web not only stems bleeding by exposing the maximum area of blood to the air but also by having the effect of a localised mini thrombosis in causing local clotting. Add that to the antiseptic qualities, and our ancestors weren't such fools. Even Shakespeare, in *A Midsummer Night's Dream* lets Bottom say, 'Good Master Cobweb, if I cut my finger, I shall make bold with you.'

The countryside is stuffed with similar truths and half-truths. One old Staffordshire cure for whooping cough (chin cough as it used to be called) was to go and find a blackberry bush which had runners long enough for the tips to grow into the ground several yards from the main bush. This resulted in long strands of prickly tendrils which were rooted at both ends so that the briar formed an arch which could be pulled two or three feet from the ground. The child was taken here at first light and passed through the spiny loop while his mother chanted: 'Over briar, under briar, we will leave the chin cough here.' If this was done three times, the cure was said to be certain.

Well, it wasn't as daft as it sounded! One of the factors that alleviated the cough was the sudden shock of cold air on the lungs so that going out at dawn and being shoved through a blackberry bush made the child bellow like a bull – and suck in copious drafts of cold air in the process. The half-truth in the story was that it was the trip at dawn, and the incentive to take great gulps of cold air that did the trick. It would probably have worked as well with honeysuckle as with briar!

One of the few holidays I have really enjoyed was taken in the wild west of Ireland in Connemara. The hotel had once been a gracious country house, the food was good and the rooms large and comfortable.

To top it off, the weather was perfect and we slept with the bedroom windows wide open so we were awakened to the song of birds.

As things turned out, we were awakened long before the birds got their heads from under their wings. In the middle of the night my wife pointed out, in no uncertain terms, that we were not the only inhabitants of that room. Half asleep and very bad tempered, I rolled over to listen. Sure enough, there *was* something. Something that quietly rustled, making far less noise than anything but a professional burglar, rifling through pockets and handbags.

I tried to locate precisely where he was, with the idea of leaping out of bed and getting my blow in first – and hitting him where it would do him least good. However, the sound never came from quite the same place twice. It was as if some ghost were flittering round the room, making no more than a whisper of sound as he passed. I stuck it as long as I could – and then I switched on the light, having loosened the bed clothes so that I had maximum mobility.

I needn't have worried. It was a magnificent long-eared bat quartering the room for the mosquitoes that would otherwise have preyed on us. I lay back in bed and marvelled at his acrobatics, saying that it was worth all the trouble of plodding right across Ireland for that one exhibition.

My wife did not agree. From deep under the bedclothes, where she had retreated, she demanded that my bat should be banished. And that I should take steps to see that he stayed banished by closing the window. Tight. However, the bat delighted me further by hanging upside down from a crack in the ceiling that didn't seem large enough to give a foothold for a fly. The exhibition was the best part of the holiday for me.

The superstition that bats get stuck in women's hair has been dispelled, once and for all, by Dilys Breese, the producer of the natural history programme 'Living World'. She placed a bat in her long black hair – and it flew away as fast as its wings would carry it.

33. Fighting Dogs Win The Day

Dog fighting is a ferocious business. It was first made illegal in 1835, not because of the cruelty but because it attracted disorderly throngs of ruffians. It was carried on surreptitiously until the 1911 Cruelty to Animals Act, which also forbade cock fighting and other 'baiting' sports. This Act was fairly successful but, even so, organised dog fighting was still quite common up to the end of the last war, especially in the Black Country where I was brought up. It is still said to be rife in the West Country.

My childhood ambitions were to own a Stafford bull terrier, not because I had any ambitions to see him fight, because my dogs have always been inseparable friends, but simply because I liked the men to whom such a dog would be an introduction. My old man would have none of it!

So I didn't have a fighting dog until I was earning my own living. But I spent thirty shillings of my first week's wages on a bull terrier pup, bred by the chap on the next machine to me. His name was Grip and, although wild horses wouldn't have forced me to allow him to fight, he was a superb ratting dog and several times killed more than a hundred rats in a day and, twice, more than a thousand in a year.

Dog fighting was a horrific 'sport'. Two dogs were carefully matched at equal weights and allowed to fight in a dog-pit which, for security reasons, was never in the same place twice. It might be in the cellar of a pub, the back bedroom of a house, or a hollow among the spoil banks of worked-out collieries. One famous battle was fought in the unlikely venue of a chapel.

All that was necessary was a square or circle about ten feet across, a handler for each dog and a referee to decide the winner. The owners were allowed to 'taste' the dogs of their opponents to satisfy themselves that the other dog had not been daubed with acid or some other substance to deter his rival from biting him. There was more gamesmanship than sport about the pastime! Then the dogs were loosed in the pit and immediately went into a deadly clinch. A round lasted until the dogs were so exhausted that they let go their holds; there was then a minute's respite for sponging down. They continued until one couldn't or wouldn't continue at the beginning of the next round. Quite often, neither recovered.

By the end of the last war, public opinion was strong enough to encourage informers to put police wise in time to stop the fights and arrest the men who conducted them. I am happy to say that the weight of public opinion, efficient police and RSPCA men wiped out dog fighting in the Midlands. Stafford bull terriers were relegated to the show ring and recognised as a breed by the Kennel Club. As so often happens with dogs bred for exhibition, their original points were exaggerated so that they became shorter legged and more barrel-chested, with heads which looked like old-fashioned bull dogs in sporting prints. The dog men of the black Country reckoned they wouldn't have stood a chance with the genuine bull terriers of their day.

Recent persistent rumours of secret dog fights in Devon and Cornwall have been discounted by the few old-timers who remember it in the Midlands. They say that the showmen have not only bred out the physical capacity to fight for more than a few minutes but also the will to fight as well. An aggressive dog is penalised in the show ring.

Although dog fighting happily has been wiped out in this country, it is still carried on in America. It is also illegal over there, but can only be stopped by Common Informer. The American pit bull terriers are direct descendants of our Black Country fighting dogs.

If dog fighting really is as rife in the West Country as rumour suggests, it seems more than likely that some of the American pit bull terriers have been imported to put the aggression back in the remnants of the old Stafford bull terrier breed. If this is true, the sooner the culprits are brought to book and put behind bars, the better.

34.   Giving Otters A Chance

Although I spend as much time as most in quiet places, I have only enjoyed the thrill of watching otters about three times in my life. When I was at school, I used to stay with a friend whose father was Rector of Montford, in Shropshire, and we used to wander along the banks of the Severn above Montford bridge, where the river crosses the main A5 road. One year a bitch otter had cubs in the roots of a hollow willow tree and, for several nights we caught glimpses of them playing as the sun was going down.

Twenty years later my wife and I saw otters while we were on holiday on the rugged west coast of Ireland in County Galway. The thrill was so great that both places have been imprinted on my mind as vividly as if

Submerged except for ears, eyes and nostrils

I grew up there. So we were naturally delighted when Philip Wayre invited us to stay for a weekend at his home at Earsham near the Norfolk-Suffolk border.

Otters are threatened more seriously than almost any other species of our native wildlife, and their numbers have declined dramatically in the last fifty years. They are exceptionally shy creatures and the easy transport and greater leisure that we now enjoy have forced them out of many of their traditional haunts in search of the quiet life they find essential. Boaters, walkers and fishermen have disturbed them accidentally but none the less seriously. The poisonous pesticides, approved by the Ministry of Agriculture, have swilled off the land into streams and ditches, where they have affected the frogs and fish the otters need as prey. The result has been less available food and what food has remained has sometimes been fatally tainted with poison.

The destruction of habitat by tidy-minded river boards may well have done most damage of all. The modern craze is to dredge out the river beds to turn rivers into drains that sluice water straight to the sea. The theory is that, in wet summers, marginal marshland will be drained to provide land for additional crops to grow. In practice, the new-made drains waste water in drier years so that the benefits of drainage are probably cancelled out by the effects of drought. The effect on otters is catastrophic because, to make their drainage works economic, the river boards grub out the trees and cover along river banks and destroy the holts, or refuges, where otters hide by day and rear their cubs.

Philip Wayre is a world authority on otters and has long realised the perils they face. He and his wife are driving forces behind the Otter Trust which performs two main functions. It is encouraging people to create conditions where otters can thrive in wild and natural conditions. There is now a large area in East Anglia where landowners have agreed to prohibit otter hunting and to limit disturbance by people walking and fishing in specified otter havens. Even the arrogant water boards are being forced to take heed of the ground swell of public opinion. But otter havens are no use without otters and Philip Wayre has a natural gift for persuading shy creatures to breed in captivity.

The Otter Trust was formed to finance the study and breeding of otters from all over the world and the members of the trust can sponsor the project financially or sometimes take an active part by helping to rear cubs themselves. At the headquarters, there are a number of large enclosures where otters live and breed. Each enclosure is surrounded by netting, buried several feet into the ground, and a pool fed by constant running water. There are growing trees and welcoming cover and, for delicate foreign otters, the sleeping boxes can be electrically heated to dry them when they come in from the water.

Philip Wayre is the only man who has succeeded in persuading our native European otters to breed in captivity and he breeds cubs at the trust every year. The surplus are set free to populate the rivers and havens where he has persuaded landowners to welcome them and keep them free from disturbance.

That weekend, Jess and I saw more otter activity than in the rest of our lives put together. The otters there are fairly used to the public for, as with people, wild creatures blossom and thrive only if they enjoy a sense of security. We watched cubs playing and marvelled that they could rush over the turf and drive, full tilt, into the water, scarcely raising a ripple. As they swam underwater, a chain of bubbles rose to the surface, revealing the precise route they took, and then they surfaced, also without a tremor. They lay motionless as crocodiles, submerged except for their eyes and nostrils and, if one missed the movement as they actually broke surface, it was easy to miss them altogether so that it was us, not they, who were being watched.

A few hours spent watching in Philip Wayre's pools explains why so few folk see otters, even in the rare places where they still survive. The trust is an example of conservation at its most effective, not only for threatened species but for encouraging all who care about the modern threats to wildlife to do something about it.

35. Appleby Fair

Not everyone would like an encampment of gipsies at the bottom of his garden. I wouldn't myself.

The gipsies themselves, the genuine Romanies, are delightful people who still travel round the country, doing seasonal work on farms or in hop-yards and orchards. If they blot their copy-books, they do not find Welcome on the mat when they call again next year.

The snag is that there are all sorts of 'travellers' besides gipsies. There are itinerant scrap-tatters and rag-and-bone men; there are hangers-on from horse racing and plain fugitives from justice. All travel under the banner of 'gipsies' – and the real gipsies resent the fact that some of the others get them tarred with the same brush.

I had a wonderful opportunity to mingle with the whole range of this society when I spent the best part of a week filming Appleby Fair for the BBC series 'In the Country'.

The horses for sale are run through the crowds

Appleby Fair

The fair is the largest horse fair in Europe and about three thousand 'gipsies' camp for the best part of a week up on the hill about a mile out of town. Even the genuine gipsies are suspicious folk, because they have endured generations of public distaste through the misdeeds of the few dregs of their circle of society. It would be impossible for strangers, like me, to gain their confidence without an introduction from someone they know and respect. So I enlisted the help of a couple of friends who know me well enough to vouch for me to the dealers at Appleby Fair.

Jack Toon, from Coalville, is a marvellous seventy-six-year-old character. He has a chain of huge scrap metal yards, capable of disposing of hundreds of cars a week. He has a thriving rag business but, at heart, he is a horse and cattle dealer, well known to all my farmer neighbours who he meets at our local Uttoxeter cattle market.

The other man who was my introduction to the dealers at Appleby Fair was Bill Brough from Doncaster. He specialises in doing up dog carts and other horse-drawn vehicles from a more leisurely age and he's one of the key men at the fair because he was once bodyguard, as he puts it, to the legendary gipsy, Boswell, and he's still no mean performer with his fists.

With two such referees to vouch for me, I was home and dry. And my own love of working dogs gave me enough background knowledge to convince the genuine Romanies that I was no mug. As a result, I had a marvellous time that I wouldn't have swapped for the trendiest holiday in more fashionable resorts. It is another world. Some of the trailers that the travellers live in cost upwards of £20,000, and they are stuffed with treasures of china and cut glass that many a museum would envy. Nobody bothers about cheque books or credit cards for the simple reason that they carry thousands of pounds in their back pockets and their horses are regarded as bank balances on the hoof.

They will start to fight at the drop of a hat, so there is a strong police presence to see that things don't get out of hand. But the police are very sensible and clever. They do not harass them or interfere unless they get rough with members of the public. A senior policeman told me that, when they do have to run one in, they make him empty his pockets to make an inventory of his possessions. It is not uncommon for them to tip £3,000 to £5,000 out of their pockets, and one last year had no less than £10,000 on him. Buying and selling everything for cash and having no fixed address means that they are strangers to the taxman. Lucky chaps.

There is no sale ring to display the horses at Appleby, and no auctioneer to take a cut. They just run them up and down through the crowds and anyone too slow to get out of the way gets knocked down. Bill Brough took me with him when he sold his horse and the experience of going flat out through a densely-packed crowd with a nag that was never quite under control was a nightmare that will haunt me for years.

All but two of the pubs in the town close, though I gather that one of the visitors always calls round next day with a fistful of cash to repair the damage if the place has got broken up a bit. But I spent a very happy evening in one of these pubs, though I was glad to be sitting with Jack Toon, as perfect strangers might not have been too welcome by the time things hotted up towards the end of a roisterous session. It was the perfect end to a delightfully offbeat break.

36.   The Hens' Miracle

If you think that a lifetime's close relationship with hens has taught me all there is to know about them, you would be wrong. I was shattered to discover, the other morning, that I was not even certain of the mechanics involved in the primitive process of laying an egg!

I always feed the hens either immediately before or immediately after breakfast, depending on what time the mornings get light: in November I breakfast first and then attend to the poultry. Even so, it was so dismal and dark when I got in the hen pen that morning that some of the birds were still having a lie-in, or sit-on?, their perches when I turned up with their grub.

On brighter days, they would have been queueing up at the nest boxes to deposit their oval offerings before jumping down to scratch in the straw litter for corn that I scatter there to encourage them to exercise. My wife wanted half a dozen eggs to give to a friend and all I could find were five, with one hen settled comfortably on her nest, crooning to herself the chortling song that is the prelude to successful egg production. So I hung around and waited and, to pass the time, I pondered on which end of the egg would appear first, the pointed end or the blunt? Prospects for solving the puzzle seemed poor, because she was sitting so comfortably that there seemed little chance of observing the actual arrival of the egg.

Just as I was giving up hope, she got up into a crouching posture, and chortling to herself, turned directly towards me so that her business end was totally obscured. One of the pleasures of keeping stock is that constant contact builds up such mutual trust that the shyest creatures grow tame. So I slid my hand gently beneath her – and she obligingly deposited her egg directly into my hand so that I was able to withdraw my prize in precisely the position in which it was presented.

It's easy to be wise after the event, of course, but I was rather surprised to discover that the egg had not appeared pointed end first, which I had imagined would incur the least discomfort. It arrived blunt end first and, when you think of the mechanics, it is obvious that gentle pressure on the long-wedge shaped side would be the best way of expelling it.

Having been troubled at times by hens that laid eggs with soft shells, I already knew that the shell does not harden after it has been laid, though that too might seem a comfortable idea. But hens need a lot of limestone grit in their diet, which is converted to make the hard shells of their eggs, and soft shells usually occur either when the hen is so productive that her shell-making mechanism does not keep pace with her output, or simply because ignorant owners neglect to put lime in her food.

The egg that was literally laid into the palm of my hand was slightly lubricated – but very hard. As an example of sheer craftsmanship it is so miraculous that the cleverest boffins simply cannot compete.

One of the party tricks of my student days, with which I won scores of pints of ale in bets, was to wager that nobody in the room was strong enough to break an egg by pressing the two ends between the palms of his hands. Ignorant fellows, who knew no better, simply took this as a spoof to get them to press an egg rashly until it broke and splattered them with gooey white and yolk. So the trick was to invite them to spatter the challenger, who would hold an egg limply between his hands and allow his fellow wagerer to apply as much pressure as he could so that, when the egg did explode under the pressure, the chap who issued the challenge would get drenched.

The plain fact is that, provided the shell is initially sound and not cracked, it will stand full pressure on its ends by the strongest man, and I never lost the bet. Scientists have calculated that, for its thickness, an egg shell is far stronger than the most sophisticated concrete building and that the curvature of its form could not be excelled for strength by human designers with the latest computers and equipment.

Add to that the fact that a common hen's egg is porous enough to allow a developing chick to get vital oxygen through the shell, robust enough to stand being shuffled round during incubation, yet delicate enough for a tiny chick to chip its way out to hatch, and it will dawn on you that you consume a miracle every time you have bacon-and-eggs for breakfast.

37.   A Quiet Christmas

It makes no odds to me whether we have a white Christmas, a green one or if it buckets down with rain. I shall enjoy whichever it is! I am content to leave my friends to hit the high spots by staying in hotels. Party games and mountains of food, soused in some foreign sauce by continental chefs mean nothing to me. I prefer simple home-cooked grub. And although we reared a couple of grand geese this year, we shall eat our Christmas dinner from a turkey fed and reared on the farm of a neighbour.

I like strangers as individuals because I am always interested to delve under the surface in conversation, to see what makes them tick. The most unlikely folk are often the most interesting when you get to know them. But the superficial bonhomie of crowds trying to be festive makes me long for the solitude of lonely places. I hate having to elbow and shove to get served at bar counters or to make an ass of myself playing party games.

So nobody will cross our threshold this Christmas who doesn't know – and, I hope, like! – everyone else. And I shan't set foot off the place.

One of the joys, as well as the chores of keeping livestock is that it provides a cast-iron excuse for not leaving it, and for sneaking off to tend it when pressures threaten. Hens have to be fed and watered and shut up, safe from foxes at night. The dogs demand walks, as well as food and comfort by the fire. Most of the relatives and friends who share Christmas with us happen to be females and, as I do not subscribe to Womens' Lib, the washing-up falls neatly into their lap. When boring jobs loom on the horizon, I suddenly discover that one of the pheasant feeders down in the wood needs topping up. Or the water in the fowl pen may have frozen. Or the deer may need a bale of hay.

If all else fails, I give a tiny sibilant whistle that is not audible to human ears. The dogs can hear it, though, for it is our secret signal that I am going for a walk. As if by magic, Tick, my pointer, leaps from her place in the centre of the hearth-rug and dances in front of me, her tail apparently wagging her body instead of the other way round. Belle, the

119

Alsatian, who sleeps on the rug round the corner of the chimney-piece, joins in and leaves no doubt that I shall fail to attend to her urgent needs at my peril.

Feigning reluctance, I stretch and yawn and complain that I had better let the dogs out – before it is too late. When we return, the washing-up is done.

Don't assume from that that I'm a skiver who dodges *all* the work. Feminine hands, with manicured nails, prefer soapsuddy water to thawing out drinking troughs and muddy fowl pens. And the nicest wenches get narrow-minded if asked to feed the ferrets. One of the pleasures of living on the edge of a wood is that we can toast our toes by open log fires without having to dig deep in our pockets to pay for the logs we burn. But those logs have to be split, so the women and I have an amicable division of labour and my sole contact with household chores is splitting the logs and laying the fire.

While the turkey is cooking, the dogs and I go up the wood. Commercial Christmas cards have conditioned our minds to the myth that the countryside is at its most beautiful only for a white Christmas. For me the trees are as attractive in sheeting rain as in any other weather. You can't see the real shape and form of a tree when it is swathed in leaves and, at this time of year, the delicate tracery of twigs and branches against a leaden sky puts to shame the most sophisticated lace devised by man, especially when the silhouette is softened by mist.

The countryside is never more silent than on Christmas Day, either. Farmers have fed and milked their cows and shepherds have checked their flocks. They have gone indoors by midday to play with the kids or to have a drink before carving the turkey. More sociable souls migrate to the local.

City slickers might complain of mud and rain down their necks, or their fingers might tingle with 'hot-ache'. But when we go for a winter walk, we see tiny leaves of honeysuckle and hazel catkins as budding promises of spring. With luck we shall see a heron surveying for possible nesting sites. The main flock will not congregate here till February, but I often see the first outrider coming to scout here on one of the days of the Christmas holiday.

I like the animals to have a good Christmas too, so I put out a bucket of corn as well as hay for the deer and a bowl of household scraps in the

Taking the dogs for a walk

hen pen. The guinea pigs have an extra carrot and the turkey giblets elevate the dogs' bowl from a dinner to a feast. We don't do too badly either. Simple, home-cooked food and our own sloe gin to top it off. A log fire to drowse by, with the dogs to share our pleasure so that canine and human company are equally agreeable.

121

38. 'Here Is The Heron Forecast'

The weatherman on the wireless rabbited on interminably about his charts and space satellites. He was saying that there 'might' be snow in Scotland and a few flurries down the east coast, but he didn't stick out his neck and say what it was going to be like in the Midlands.

I thought it was more accurate – and cheaper – in grand-mother's day when she made predictions from the throbbing of her corns! I took my cue of snow to come from the herons. The first arrivals usually turn up around Christmas to stake their claims for the five-star nesting sites and there is often quite a colony of them settled by mid-January,

A grey heron moves to a new feeding ground

quarrelling loudly and collecting at least a token quantity of nesting material. However, I haven't seen a heron in our wood since the last of the nesting colony dispersed about the beginning of September.

This can only mean that there has been some major catastrophe, some mass slaughter by shooters or poisonous pesticides – or that they are simply staying away for reasons of their own. Years ago, I should have been very worried, but past experience has sometimes shown that they are late arriving when there is dirty weather to come. They seem to be able to sense the onset of hard weather. I have no idea how they do this because, judging by human experience, it is impossible.

Apart from lucky stabs, the boffins in our meteorological office can't tell for certain what it will do tomorrow, let alone give a long-term forecast. So, how do the birds know better? Whatever the answer is, the fact is that our herons are exceptionally late in returning to their breeding sites this year and I shall be surprised if there is not some foul weather in the pipeline. If the weatherman wants to make a long-term forecast, he will disregard them at his peril.

Between now and about the beginning of March, or right into April in exceptional winters like 1947 and 1963, the weather can be critical for many animals and birds. Herons, for example, catch fish, frogs, moles and water rats for their food and when the water is armour-plated with a thick sheet of ice, there is no way they can spear a fish except in the strongest running water. And fish instinctively seek deep water at such times because it is safer there.

Kingfishers are in the same plight and both species die off by the dozen in the sort of winters our herons seem to fear. Woodpeckers, which have abnormally long tongues, get them frost-bitten when they are probing the tiny tunnels made in trees by the maggots of wood-boring beetles.

Even large creatures, like deer, give signs for those with eyes to see that winter is no picnic. When they change their coats in spring, they take weeks about it, presumably because they have not yet regained condition after feeding on grass and leaves that are as dried as hay but do not contain the nourishment. When they cast their summer coats and change to darker coats for winter, they are in such fine fettle that the whole process is over within about half the time.

In theory, whole species *should* be wiped out by the sort of winters we

123

experienced in 1947 and 1963, but the fact is that their populations recovered within a few years because they have evolved various ways of surviving. Frogs, toads, fish and many insects lay literally thousands of eggs so that although the odds against survival of any one youngster are astronomical, they are equally great that the catastrophe won't wipe out every last one.

It isn't just luck that the few odd survivors don't suffer the fate of the majority. It is often because they are the freaks, or genetic sports, which have evolved a characteristic that happens to help against the conditions that annihilated their relatives. Perhaps it is a thicker coat, or the ability to hibernate and sleep through cold spells. Birds, like wrens, which are so small that they cannot conserve enough body heat to sustain life through a night of exceptional frost, have developed the instinct to roost snuggled in large groups. They keep each other warm as a community when they would have perished individually. On top of that, they lay many eggs and have exceptionally large broods, to lengthen the odds that at least some will survive.

Nature may be wasteful and profligate, but she is really ruthlessly efficient. All selective breeding is a matter of compromise, and the single purpose for which Nature is prepared to sacrifice everything else is the survival of the species. She is prepared to put up with funny-looking creatures, like hedgehogs, hyperspecialists like swifts which spend almost all their lives on the wing, catching flies, and the extravagance of frogs, which spawn thousands of eggs for a couple of so to reproduce.

Our selective stockmanship too often sacrifices vitality for unnaturally high production of eggs, milk or meat. Such diseases as fowl pest, bovine TB and foot-and-mouth disease do for domestic stock what climatic freaks do in the wild. The cleverest of our boffins are still unable to compete with Nature!

39. Unwelcome Guests

There is no one more bumptious than a bumptious bureaucrat. I was recently landed in a rather dull party, where most of the guests were big fish in little pools, the biggest bore of them all being some sort of big shot on a water board. I couldn't help ribbing him about the proliferation of water board vans that litter the countryside and the resultant escalating charges. The more annoyed he got, the more bombastic he became.

In order to put me in my place, he announced that, whatever I thought about it, he could come on my land whenever he liked. When I told him, equally firmly, that he couldn't, he produced from his pocket a pass, with his photograph on it, which he claimed entitled him to come, without notice, to make an inspection to satisfy himself that I wasn't breaking any of his regulations. I explained that my Alsatian can neither read passes nor recognise photographs! It brought the house down and pricked his pomposity, but I fear that my success was more in theory than in practice.

To discover just how starry-eyed I was, I asked the Country Land-owners' Association to send me their leaflet *Rights of Entry on Land*. It is a daunting document covering no less than eight pages of closely-typed foolscap. The Secretary of State for the Environment can send anyone he chooses on to your land to make investigations if he believes it contains an ancient monument, though he must obtain your consent if he wants to make excavations.

It says nothing about consequences if you tell him to get lost or if you leave your Alsatian loose. If you kick out the man from the electricity board because he wants to survey for a power line or sub-station or similar monstrosity, you can be hauled before the beak and relieved of twenty quid. The gas and electricity men can come and check if you are fiddling the meter whenever they like, but that seems fair enough. If you refuse to allow the man who wants to survey possible footpaths or bridleways, the penalty is not £20, but £50. Pest officers can come and kill your rabbits, hares, deer, foxes, moles and certain birds *and* destroy

125

their breeding places and cover, if the Ministry of Agriculture thinks they might be a nuisance. They can check your rats, mice, badgers, weeds and caravan sites, and the little man at the party can 'inspect and survey land for the purpose of deciding whether and in what manner the functions of the water authority are to be performed as well as rights of entry for performing those functions'.

Shades of the days when an Englishman's home was his castle! All this may well be changed in the near future – for the worse. The Wildlife and Countryside Bill, currently on its way through Parliament, seeks to make compromises which will satisfy all interests in the countryside. This is obviously utterly impractical because so many interests are completely opposite that to satisfy one faction it is inevitable that it will antagonise the other.

The Bill attempts the impossible by trying to placate all sides at the same time. The promoters are on a hiding to nothing and it would surely be wiser to encourage farmers on marginal land, which is often the most beautiful, to treat visitors as a cash crop by charging them for the privilege of enjoying their leisure on their farms. Shooting men and fishermen already pay for their sport and even bird watchers pay for permits to go on the land.

Why should casual visitors be treated any differently? If they paid for the privilege of enjoying themselves on other people's land, some of them would treat it with more respect – and it would be far easier to welcome invited guests than it is to put up with the arrogance of those who boast they have a pass – or 'right'!

40.   Winter Sport

Sentimentalists who regard all creatures as furry friends would have been disillusioned by the behaviour of our deer in snow. Waking last weekend to find eight inches unscheduled by the weatherman, I put out a bale of sweet hay where we could watch it through the windows.

Farmers, feeding sheep or cattle, would have broken the bale up and dumped it in piles several yards apart. They know from experience that domestic stock has a pecking-order as clearly defined as the class sytem in any status-conscious society. Only by spreading around the available feed points is it possible to prevent the four-legged bully-boys from using their superior clout to scoff the lot.

Although I am fully aware of this, I still fell for the illusion that deer are gentle, noble beasts that know how to behave in a more civilised way than thugs in our society. From a purely practical point of view, it seemed silly to break up the bale into small piles which would quickly get soaked and buried in the snow.

Honey, my old white doe, found it first and shook a few wisps out of the bale before starting to tuck in. Three of her daughters came up, including the fawn that she had last year, but they didn't get a look-in. As soon as they came within grabbing distance of the feast she was sampling, she turned on them and drove them off. Last year's fawn, which is scarcely weaned, was obviously hurt and offended. She went off in a huff.

Honey didn't have it all her own way for very long. One of the bucks saw the deer feeding and came up to examine the menu. He lowered his head and sent them all skittering in every direction. Then he settled down for a leisurely feed. The one mistake he made was in thinking that he was Lord of Creation. Although I don't claim the title myself, I demonstrated that I was, at least, higher in life's pecking-order. I went out, chivvied him off and redistributed the hay in a row of small piles where he could only monopolise one at a time and the lesser fry could tuck in to the rest.

The fairly heavy fall of snow, with no wind, had a magical effect on the wood. Everywhere seemed utterly silent. But, just as the thick blanket stifles sound, it accentuates the slightest movement. A fox, crossing a field half a mile away, would have been invisible against a dark background but would now be silhouetted as sharply as if he had been underlined in a picture. Even more illuminating is a walk round the boundaries of the wood the following day. Although nearly all animals are creatures of very fixed habits, snow gives away clues to their movements that would otherwise be difficult to detect. However, after snow, the significance of every anonymous gap in the fence suddenly grows clear.

Rabbits pass through selected holes in the wire netting. Although the mesh of sheep netting round part of the wood is all four inches in diameter, rabbits are very selective about the precise mesh they use. Here and there I saw that a fox had passed and one mound of roots I

Deer feeding in the snow at Goat Lodge

thought deserted had been visited by a badger. Tracks which have so obviously been used in snow will still be used when it has gone.

My greatest surprise came from the most unlikely source. My ferrets sleep in a warm box in one of the outbuildings, which is entered through a drain pipe cemented through the wall. They emerge into a large wire-netting enclosure which, in its time, has served as the run to a dog kennel, the aviary where I rehabilitated Fred, the orphan barn owl, and now its present use as a ferret run.

Ignorant people think that ferrets are all fierce, smell foul and are the most unattractive form of small mammal. The poor wretches, doomed to life imprisonment in miserable hutches that are rarely cleaned out, may well fit the description, but mine do not.

Ferrets are as fastidious as their relatives the badgers and keep themselves scrupulously clean if their living conditions allow it. They are also as playful as badgers and chase each other round and round their spacious run with the agility of squirrels. One of them discovered that it is great fun to dig its nose in the soft snow and push it ahead like a miniature snow plough. The others joined in and the fluffy snowball on the ferret's nose grew until it was too big to push. The others helped and, when they could no longer push it, they rolled it and, as they rolled it, it gradually grew in size. The ferrets contented themselves with shoving their snowball around until it was almost as big as a football and they could no longer move it, then they grew bored.

All naturalists know that otters love playing in the snow and make slides which they chase each other down time after time. I have never seen this behaviour mentioned with badgers, but my tame badger often played in snow and I have a photograph of a slide he made.

My ferrets are first cross with a wild polecat, and all are related to badgers and otters, but I have never heard of polecats playing in the snow so that the discovery that mine loved it may well have broken new ground. Badgers, ferrets and otters are all related; they smell vaguely alike and their voices are similar. Therefore, I should not have been surprised that they enjoyed the same sort of games. And if I find an unexpected snowball in the wood, I shall add it to the clues that warn me what to look for.

41. Discharging Death Downstream

A rhyme in an old book about Birmingham and the Black Country, describes the River Tame a century and a half ago. It says:

> The Tame is foul as foul can be,
> With sewage black as dye,
> It runs with garbage, in the wet,
> And stinks when it is dry.
> No fishes lie beneath its banks.
> There are no fish to lie!

Those were the days when the tanneries of Walsall were at their zenith, disgorging industrial filth into the river that still runs under the bridge, in the centre of the town. The sludge that resulted was spiced by satanic concoctions from countless mines and factories which made water in many of our rivers about as wholesome as the additives prescribed by medieval professional poisoners for the victims of their clients.

Plague, in the Middle Ages, was often spread by contaminated water, and at this time of year, the well-dressing ceremonies of such Derbyshire villages as Tissington are annual thanksgiving services as well as attractions for thousands of visitors who flock to see them. Beautiful floral designs recall the fact that villagers did not catch the plague because they shut themselves off from the outside world and drew their communal water supply from uncontaminated local wells.

Fears for its own safety encouraged the public to apply enough pressure on politicians to pass laws that cleaned things up a bit but, even today, some of our rivers, including the Midlands' own Tame, are nothing to be proud about. The most diligent search will still be unlikely to find many fishes lying beneath her banks, for the same reason mentioned in the rhyme. The minimum of controls removed the worst perils to human health, but the degree of pollution allowed by law is still deadly to wildlife.

Public health authorities now monitor the discharge from the factories of industrial areas so that the worst offenders now live in deep country and put wildlife in peril instead of people. Chemical pesticides used by farmers are the most popular Aunt Sallies nowadays because the havoc wreaked by such poisons as aldrin and dieldrin in the 1950s and the 1960s raised a public outcry when tens of thousands of dead birds and animals were discovered strewn all over the countryside. You don't need much imagination to be mistrustful of a chap in a mask with breathing apparatus, rubber gloves and coat and boots, squirting a fog of foul-smelling chemicals over a field of corn. If the stuff is as innocuous as he pretends, why is it necessary for him to tog himself up like a man from outer space?

Yet you would probably have no qualms about the brook downstream from a herd of cattle feeding on silage, which is the modern substitute for old-fashioned hay. The grass can be cut younger for silage than for hay because it is wilted and compressed, green, in the silage pit. It has a powerful pong, which many find distasteful, but the fact that it does smell so strong gives a clue to a chemical change and the fact is that seepage from a silage pit that finds its way to a river or stream is about as lethal to wildlife as many chemical pesticides.

Fishermen comprise one of the most powerful pressure groups in the countryside. They are not particularly active in the cause of wildlife, destroying thousands of swans and other birds, either by poisoning them with the lead shot used to sink their lines or entangling them in the tangle of broken nylon casts that litter the river banks, but anyone who threatens their sport is in for trouble.

The chaps from the Anglers' Co-operative Association are a litigious lot and will take anyone to court, from the local council who spill tar when mending the road, to a farmer spilling silage, if either pollutes fishing water. They have probably done more to clean up rivers in recent years than either conservationists or public officials. But they now have a tricky problem on their hands.

Fish farming has lately become the 'in' thing. Up and down the country, scores of people are now rearing trout and other fish, which are reared as intensively as any farm stock. They are sold direct to customers for the table, or to fishery owners for re-stocking their water for the unskilled 'sportsman' who prefers easy 'put-in-and-take-out'

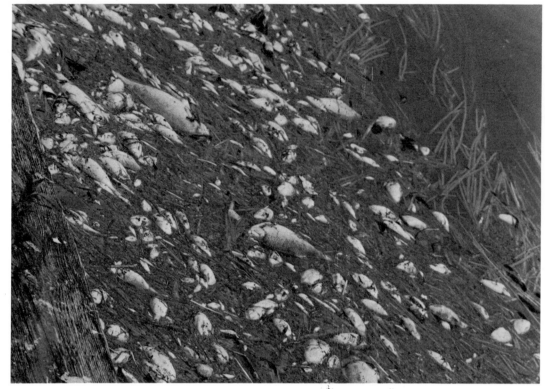

Pollution on the River Cam has terrible results

fishing to developing the skill to outwit and catch a wily, wild fish.

Thousands of tons of rearing pellets are fed to these mass-produced fish, which respond by depositing thousands of tons of excrement which is discharged downstream from the fish farm. The dangers of so much neat sewage are obvious and would raise a storm if produced by anything but fish. Fish, incidentally, can suffer from disease associated with intensive husbandry which may in turn carry infection to healthy wild stock downstream.

The National Water Council and regional water authorities are keeping their heads down and 'saying nowt'. So the ball lies with the Anglers' Co-operative Association, though it seems to be caught between two fishing interests which, for once, are in opposition. However, if someone does not grasp the nettle and bring pressure on fish farmers who are discharging death downstream, we shall hear an encore of that rhyme dedicated to the Tame.

42.   The Politics Of Leisure

My recent pessimism about the Wildlife and Countryside Bill now on a stormy passage through Parliament, has proved more than justified. Here is a Bill that should, in theory, transcend the petty wranglings of party politicians. Its aim is to protect pressured wildlife and threatened countryside so that England will still be worth living in for future generations. It would be difficult to conceive how anyone could quarrel with that.

Proof of the pudding's indigestibility is the fact that almost eight hundred amendments were tabled which would reduce it to absurdity. Some of the rifts that have been exposed among so-called country lovers seem purely selfish. As I have written on page 96, walkers and farmers are quarrelling about whether bulls should be allowed loose in fields crossed by footpaths. Dog owners even yelp at having to keep their pets on a lead in fields containing sheep.

It is a matter of small importance. As far as I am concerned they can all emasculate each other till they all begin to yodel. What does matter is the future of threatened species of wildlife and our dwindling number of rare habitats and wild places. Once gone they can never be replaced. Even here, there are fundamental differences of opinion. Farmers make their living off the land and it is vital to us, their customers, that they are able to grow enough food to feed us. Most folk would agree with that in principle. However, when it is examined in detail it becomes a matter of priorities.

A farmer with acres of swamp on his farm sees it as unproductive land and wants to take advantage of modern earth-moving equipment to drain it. Conservationists may know that rare insects or plants thrive in that particular swamp, *because* it is a swamp. If it were drained to grow a few extra potatoes or a few tons more corn, the rare species which excite the naturalists would disappear.

Who, therefore, is to decide which matters most, extra food for hungry mouths or some plant or creature that might be wiped from the face of the earth by modern methods?

The same goes for poisonous pesticides. The boffins have devised pesticides which spell death and destruction to almost every known species of pest. While they are at it, they also annihilate myriads of plants and insects which are not pests. Anyway, who is to define what is and what is not a pest. Wild flowers, in the wrong place, are treated as weeds. The satanic brews that are so devastating are peddled openly by the Ministry of Agriculture and Fisheries in its *Approved Products for Farmers and Growers.* *

The differences of opinion between farmers and conservationists are understandable. Food for people is arguably as powerful an argument as whether it is right to sacrifice other species to save our own. However, killing rarities to improve the quality of sport is another matter. Shooting men have tarnished their image by employing game keepers to 'control' what they have been pleased to describe as vermin. The more barbaric types of trap, notably the gin trap, have been outlawed. But modern self-lock snares often mutilate as badly, causing agonising deaths, as protracted as any caused by a gin. Such species as rats and rabbits liable to catastrophic population explosions and immense damage to food and crops obviously need their numbers curtailed.

Most people would agree that there are some species of plant, animal and bird in danger which should have legal protection. It follows that circumstances may arise when even these creatures may grow too numerous or be harmful locally, so it might be necessary to control their numbers. The Bill would provide a list of protected species and allow even those to be controlled under licence.

The problem is, who would issue the licence? A powerful pressure group insists that licences should be granted by officials of the Ministry of Agriculture. God forbid! No department has a worse record with wildlife. When rats acquired an immunity to the poison Warfarin, the bench-bound boffins at the Ministry were so ignorant that they wasted thousands of pounds trying to exterminate all the rats near Craven Arms, in Shropshire, where the outbreak of resistant rats occurred. Any competent naturalist, who knew what went on in the field as well as the lab., could have told them that, as fast as you clear any attractive area of

* *see also* No. 12

habitat of a species, it refills from the surrounding land as surely as water finds its own level.

They have made the same stupid mistake with badgers, which they are gassing by tens of thousands in the West Country. One sett has been gassed twenty-four times because it is always repopulated. Now they are thinking of calling in the Chemical Defence Department, from Porton Down, which is more expert at annihilation. They have squandered £600,000 on a fiasco – without checking the spread of bovine TB significantly.

The Ministry of Agriculture issues licences for strychnine for poisoning moles, cyanide for badgers and alfachloralose for birds. The Ministry is a specialist in destruction, not conservation. No wonder Lord Craigton has been 'desperately unhappy throughout the Bill' which he feels has achieved absolutely nothing. Lord Melchett, the Opposition spokesman, believes that 'the interests of wildlife would be better preserved by dropping the Bill altogether'.

To allow the men from the Ministry to acquire control over our wildlife would be as lethal as the kiss of death.

AUTHOR'S NOTE – JULY 1982

When the Ministry did eventually call in the scientists from Porton Down, they got a shock. Instead of endorsing their mass extermination by cyanide gas, the scientists – who are past-masters in the art of chemical and germ warfare – produced horrific figures to show precisely how long badgers lingered before dying from various concentrations of gas. The agony could last anything from one to twenty-five minutes.

Peter Walker, Minister of Agriculture, had no alternative but to execute a humiliating U-turn in July 1982 and order his rat-catchers to suspend gassing badgers forthwith.

Surely the fact that Ministry scientists, backed by the British Veterinary Association, condoned the inhumane gassing of tens of thousands of badgers over the period of seven years has destroyed their last shreds of credibility. Their campaign does not even have the excuse that it has been effective because although they have squandered over £60,000 in the gassing operation, Bovine TB is still spreading in their area of operation.

It is thought that the reason for this is that clearing large areas of badgers simply results in uncontrolled population movements of badgers flooding in from the surrounding country to replace them, frequently from infected to 'clean' areas.

It is high time to put the matter into the more responsible hands of a department such as the Nature Conservancy Council which employs scientists with a broader knowledge of ecology and a more human approach. Advanced scientists now believe it would be quite feasible to develop an oral vaccine which could be fed in bait to badgers living near infected cattle. This would remove the suspicion that badgers might spread the disease without causing population movements.

43.   Our Bottle Tits

My wife arrived with the good tidings that we had bottle tits in the garden. In case you think that sounds unduly alcoholic, I will rephrase it. She came in to say that canbottles were nesting in the thicket in the shrubbery.

Canbottles, or bottle tits, are country names for what bird-watchers call long-tailed tits and learned ornithologists insist on calling by their Latin name of *Aegithalos caudatus rosaceus*. A rose by any other name is just as sweet – and so is a long-tailed tit.

The fact is that the names 'canbottle' and 'bottle tit' do not really refer to the bird at all, but to the nest it builds. It is a miracle of delicate

The long-tailed tit has an elfin beauty all of its own

construction because it is built of tiny strands of moss, laid in place from the inside of the nest and bound together with cobwebs. The whole nest is woven into the twigs of a dense thorn, gorse bush or other thick shrub. It is built in an oval shape, with the entrance at the top, which gives the bird the name of bottle tit or canbottle. The superb craftsmanship does not end with the framework of moss and cobwebs. Interior decoration is a lining of feathers, blended smooth as a lady's hat, and it is by no means uncommon for a pair of tits to use two thousand feathers for the interior.

As you might expect with such avian artists, the birds have an elfin beauty all their own. Although they are tiny creatures, they look larger because they have narrow tails which are longer than their bodies. When they are flying, these long tails stream out behind them, and even a slight breeze will slew them off course. They remind me of miniature helicopters. Head and underparts are off-white, with dull black bands on back and wings. But there are delicate bands of pink on shoulders and underparts, to which the *rosaceus* in their Latin name obviously refers.

Apart from the breeding season, canbottles are sociable little birds. I often see them in the wood in winter in parties of anything up to twenty, and they join with flocks of commoner tits. We get quite a few goldcrests, which are even smaller than common wrens, that also like to join the party. They are usually high in the tops of the birch trees, flitting across the wood as they feed on birch seeds and any spiders, midges or insects they can find. The first indication that they are there is usually a subdued, but high-pitched twittering in the tree-tops. Then they leap-frog past each other as they compete to be first at the next course of their living larder.

However, when the flocks split up as the breeding season approaches, they grow secretive and hard to see. Being so tiny, they are particularly hit by hard winters because their bodies are not big enough to store enough heat to sustain them overnight in really severe frosts. Sometimes, quite large parties crowd into a communal roost in such weather to keep each other warm, as wrens do. But even so, they are always rare after bad winters.

Bottle tits are such shy and solitary birds when breeding that I don't flatter myself that they would have chosen our garden if there had been enough suitable secret places in the wood. Now that they have come, they are more than welcome, but I shall have to take steps to protect them from predators, especially jays and magpies. Suffering as badly as they do in hard winters, it is vital for the survival of their species to have as large families as possible.

They lay anything up to a dozen eggs, which take about sixteen days to hatch, and families of that size take a mighty lot of feeding. The young get very hungry as they approach full size and as they grow more hungry, the more loudly they scream for their food. This doubtless spurs the old birds to greater efforts – but it also gives away the position of their perfectly-camouflaged nest. Magpies, crows and jays not only have sharp eyes, but they sit around listening a lot as well. When they hear young birds screaming for food, they move gradually nearer to the source of the sound, watching for parents to return with food. The combination of patience with sharp eyes and ears locates the predator's next meal – and the most beautifully-woven cobwebs, horsehair and moss is no defence.

I know all too well that the chances of survival for our nest of bottle tits are pretty slim – unless my rifle stops the local magpies in their tracks.

44. Let Sheep Graze Over My Grave

The parishioners of a village near Malvern have started to bleat about sheep in the churchyard. About a year ago, growing wages wrote off the chances of finding the cash to keep the place as professionally trim as fond memories for the departed demand. Ancient, jutting gravestones are difficult obstacles for amateurs to negotiate with motor mowers; and scythes and bill-hooks belong to past generations. Standards were slipping until the suggestion was made to introduce a gang of Nature's grass-cutters in the guise of a flock of sheep.

Nothing looks neater than the well-barbered sward that grows beneath the cloven hooves of healthy sheep. Supine headstones, the edges of uneven paths and the steepest banks are equally acceptable dining-tables to them. The roughest burial grounds can soon be tamed to bowling green perfection.

The alternatives are horrific. Churchyards either grow into untamed jungles of elderberry and nettles and brambles. Or, as too often happens, some unimaginative vicar with a tiny, tidy mind sanctions a scheme to level the graves and turn the place into a featureless, flat field which can be mown like a public park.

That is the fate that apparently threatens this Worcestershire village. Although the acre of rough ground where the sheep were paddocked looks better, they also had access to wander over some graves. One parishioner, for whom the problem may be growing imminent, said that sheep are messy things and that to have them wandering over the graves may distress relatives.

I suppose it's a matter of taste, but when I finally tumble off my perch, I would rather be covered by a lush blanket of sheep-shorn grass than a neglected mat of weeds, or horrific artificial flowers entombed in sterile glass.

In these times of insecurity, when the odds against tomorrow arriving seem depressingly short, tangible evidence of ancestors, who must have had rough patches as well as smooth, is very comforting. It is never safe to make a derogatory remark about any native of our village, for it is a pound to a gooseberry that the object of your criticism will turn out to be a relation of the chap to whom you are talking. A visit to the churchyard, a few years ago, would have confirmed the point. The same names appeared on gravestones for generation after generation; the names of butchers and bakers, farmers and publicans, were carved, in loving letters, on the headstones.

But we live in an age of change which, all too often, is different rather than better. New whizzkid vicars thought otherwise and started landscaping their churchyards so that they could be mechanically cultivated. In my view, they grubbed up history with the gravestones they removed. And strangers, calling at their churchyard in the hopes of discovering evidence of ancestors linking them to the solid past, could now be disappointed.

The modern fashion is for churchyards to be as uniform and characterless as the trendy traffic-free shopping precincts in every town, where supermarkets and chain stores, computerised to the eyebrows, have sent generations of honest tradesmen up the spout.

So when it was proposed to desecrate our churchyard (as I regarded it), I told the vicar what I thought. His reply was perfectly reasonable. He said that, although he could see that the sheep might barber the grass, the bereaved might object if they scoffed the flowers that they had put in vases on the graves.

However, sheep are easy to fold. The modern way is to erect a roll of sheep wire netting round the paddock to be grazed, and support it with iron stakes that are easy to erect and move. By doing this in fields of grass, the farmer can ensure that each strip of grass is completely grazed down before they are moved to the next. When they are moved, the boundary of their new paddock prevents them from returning to the strip they have left.

So my idea for a churchyard would be to get a friendly farmer to put up a temporary fence and flood the specified area with so many sheep that they would bite off the grass within a few days – and be gone. Flowers would only have to be lifted for the short time they were there and when they were gone, the whole place would be neat as a new pin.

45. Morning Glory At Our Pit 'Ole

The plan hanging in my study describes the pool at the far end of the wood as Primrose Dell. My friends from the Black Country would call it 'a bit of a pit 'ole.'

Both would be right, though the water has not settled as a result of mining subsidence, as the Black Country 'swags' of my youth were formed. The pit that forms Primrose Dell was dug out, in generations past, by men with picks and shovels winning marl to spread on the land. Our heavy clay is very acid but there are odd pockets of marl which contains free lime, which is wonderful for sweetening the soil. Large-scale maps show dozens of these old marl pits in our part of the country and, when the marl had been dug and spread, the holes left soon filled with water.

Our 'pit 'ole' is only about as big as a couple of tennis courts with three sides twenty or thirty feet deep. It is shaped like a basin with four or five feet of water in the bottom. The scars the labourers left have long since healed over and are clothed in sweet grass, which the deer graze to the texture of a trim lawn. Clumps of primroses cascade down the steep sides of the dell, punctuated by cowslips, some of which cross-pollinate the primroses to produce hybrid oxslips. It always seems strange to me that flowers of such purity are not as prim as their name implies and that they are no better than they should be, but fall for the temptation of an illicit romp as easily as mere mortals!

The charms of the dell are not confined to the primrose family. There are also wild violets, kingcups, ladysmocks and wood anemones, or 'wind flowers', which bow decorously in the slightest breeze. When they are over, there will be a mat of giant mare's tail, whose primitive ancestors were crushed and fossilised to make the coalfields that lie under so much of the Midlands.

In the last twenty years, the sides of the dell have sprouted dense clumps of hawthorn and blackthorn that are perfect, prickly nesting

141

cover for scores of songbirds. Linnets, warblers and tree pipits sound off in chorus, but the scarcest avian aristocrat cannot compete, for my money, with the common robins and blackbirds that also live in the dell.

I love to go there for an hour at sunset, though the midges that breed in the water and lie in wait in the bushes sometimes make me question my own sanity for exposing myself to their attacks. The best time of all is the hour after dawn, because the cool morning air has tamed the pestilent insects and the bird song is at its heavenly best.

I was down there at first light the other morning and a hare was grazing on a clover patch down by the water's edge. The wind was blowing in my direction, so that she didn't sense that I was there, and she gradually grazed nearer and nearer until I could see the individual beads of dew collecting from the grasses on her coat. Sitting erect on her

A coot makes ripples in Primrose Dell

haunches to perform her toilet, she groomed every bead of moisture from her fur until her coat shone as sleek as the finest satin.

I know of nothing so peaceful as to be alone in such a quiet spot where obtrusive, man-made noises of the day have not yet started; where time does not seem to matter and everything is as it was in our ancestors' time.

I say it's peaceful to be alone, but the fact is that I rarely am alone for the dogs nearly always accompany me. I have trained them to be absolutely steady. At the faintest hiss of 'Down' or 'Stay', they freeze into immobility and they are happy to remain as immobile as I am for as long as I like.

They are both marvellous ratters and will catch vermin as expertly as the best bull terrier, but they never flicked an eyelid as the hare approached that morning, and they would no more think of raising their hackles or licking their chops at deer or pheasants or even rabbits without permission.

As the hare loped off across my boundary into a field of young corn, she was replaced by the young muntjac deer which is the daughter of the pair I reared by hand. We rarely see this kid, which is as wild as her mother is tame. It came mincing along over the edge of the dell quite oblivious of our presence and both dogs sat still as statues. The deer passed within ten yards without even suspecting the presence of what could so easily have been mortal enemies.

Half an hour's patient wait in our pit 'ole is worth a day's tramp in strange places!

46. Our Tap Ran Dry At Milking Time

When we bought our cottage, almost twenty years ago, the facilities were pretty basic. There was neither electricity nor gas, lighting was by paraffin lamps and the cooking was done on an old coal stove that had a tank on one side to provide hot water. This was not all it was cracked up to be because there was no piped supply. If you forgot to keep it filled, the whole thing glowed red hot.

There was one stark cold tap over the sink, but whoever installed it had overlooked the small matter of drainage, so that the overflow poked through the scullery wall and emptied on to a flower bed. Until fairly recently, the only water had been from a pump in the yard that drew its supply from the well beneath. As this was within five yards of the earth privy, which was the only sanitation, the previous inhabitants must have been very tough or developed their own immunity.

We like our creature comforts so, before we moved in, we installed electricity for lighting and cooking, lavatories that flushed and emptied into a modern septic tank (there is no sewer within a mile) and water H & C, as the adverts put it. We thought we now had the best of both worlds, with all modern conveniences combined with rural seclusion.

It wasn't long before we noticed that our water pressure was sometimes good, at other times dreadful. It never actually dried up, but on Monday mornings, when the ladies were washing in the village a mile away, the cold tap was sometimes little more than a trickle. We had put large storage tanks in the roof, so that this didn't matter much if we didn't actually want to drink the stuff and we got used to a somewhat unreliable supply.

The time came when both my neighbours doubled their milking herds – and it gradually dawned on me how much cows drink. Immediately after milking, the whole herd went to their water troughs and replaced the liquid that had just been extracted for bottling at the dairy. Hygiene is essential in such enterprises so, immediately after milking is completed, the farmers wash everything down.

Our water supply faded away until nothing came out of the cold tap, not a single, sparkling drop for an hour or two on end. It got a bit frustrating! I sent for the man from the waterworks and he pointed out that both my neighbouring farmers and I got our supply across the fields from the main road a mile away. When it came over private property, apparently, it was our affair. So long as the pressure was all right when it left the public main, they couldn't care less.

My view was that if a few of the chaps swanning around in neat vans marked Severn-Trent concentrated on giving their customers value for their meter money, there would be less faulty supplies.

So we had to cope ourselves. Luckily for me, my neighbour is a helpful chap and he suggested that I take my supply before it reached him instead of after, because the drop I use would hardly be noticed from the supply he draws for his dairy. So a private contractor came and laid four or five hundred yards of modern plastic pipe of twice the diameter of the little pipe that had previously come up from the farm.

The result is dramatic. It is easy to expect a plentiful supply of clean water as a basic necessity that arrives at the touch of a tap but over the years, we had *almost* got used to having little or none for several hours at a time. When we made a cup of tea, we automatically filled the kettle for the next in case there would be none in the tap when we wanted it. Now that water arrives whenever we wish it, we are grateful for the sheer luxury. We appreciate our blessings.

But it does drive home the fact that such amenities are not just there for the taking. They have to be worked for and paid for and, all too often, some bumptious bureaucrat either has to be bypassed or chivvied into earning his keep.

A farmer friend was telling me the other day that the do-gooders are trying to stop him having an overhead powerline to supply power to his farm 'because it will spoil the view'! Whose view will it spoil? The view of a few strangers who want to go walking there on Sundays and think that the countryside should be kept as 'olde worlde' as it was in grandad's time, when men cut hay with scythes and carried their water from communal wells in buckets, supported by yokes on their necks!

The truth is that the countryside is a living entity which does not stand still. It is always changing and it always has. It was once densely wooded, with few clearings for primitive agriculture. Gradually, as the woods were cleared, they were replaced by little fields – and I expect there were those who grumbled that the wooded scenes their grandfathers loved were now a pattern of formalised crops.

Now that machines are replacing labour on the land, the little fields are making way for fields as big as little farms, for mammoth contraptions that can reap and thresh and harvest in one operation. So people complain about the disappearance of hedges that have only been part of the English scene for comparatively few centuries.

Luckily for the wildlife which loses its breeding habitat, sport has become a viable crop, so farmers are planting up odd, uneconomic patches for game coverts – which happen to be equally attractive to small birds. The change is an *on-going* process – but it is easy to forget how living standards have improved in the last generation. Electricity and piped water, which were counted luxuries then, are taken as necessities now but, having tried things the hard way, I for one appreciate my luck.

47.   The RSPB Leads
The Way

The Royal Society for the Protection of Birds is more than the bunch of starry-eyed do-gooders who too often comprise such bodies. They practise what they preach, not only by looking objectively at the troubles of those who do not like birds so much, but also by offering sound advice about ways of minimising the damage some of them do.

Julie Meyer, in her report to the RSPB, calculates that anything up to 5,500 herons are slaughtered by fish farmers on suspicion of eating their trout. Out of an estimated breeding population of only about 5,000 pairs, this means that each pair has got to rear two young to replace the devastation wreaked by fish farmers alone. Now herons are fully protected by law, so how do thousands of them get shot?

As I have so often complained, the wildlife protection laws of this country are scarcely worth the paper they are written on. What the law says is that it is illegal to trap, poison or shoot a heron 'unless the accused can prove in court of law that it was causing serious damage'. A trout farmer suffering damage to his fish, however negligent he has been in protecting them, gets away with it practically every time.

So I admire the practical approach of the RSPB for arranging a research worker to look at the problem, from the fish-farmer's angle, and then to devise ways of minimising it.

The temptations to the birds are enormous. The easiest sort of pool to fish is an earth pool, with shallow sloping sides down which the heron can wade till it reaches optimum fishing depth. Such pools may be crammed with anything up to 40,000 tame fish.

Julie Meyer's research was nothing if not thorough. The preferred size of trout she found weighed about half a pound, and in 'good' (easily fishable) trout pools, there might be anything up to forty herons, all more expert than the cleverest human fisherman. At 60p a fish, a fish farmer might lose several thousand pounds a year.

Instead of wringing their hands in anguish, the RSPB proposed more practical measures. It produced diagrams to show that pools with steeply sloping sides were difficult for herons to fish. Julie's research included experiments with various types of bird deterrents. She showed that 'bangers' – the conventional bird-scarers used by farmers – were only effective for very limited periods before the herons rumbled the fact they were only bluff and bluster. She did experiments which showed that scarecrows, streamers and flashing lights were only effective when moved frequently. She was able to convince hard-headed businessmen, as opposed to idealists with rose-tinted specs, that it was actually cheaper to deter herons scientifically than it was to pay men to shoot them.

Two strands of cord, stretched round the edge of the pool at between ten and fourteen inches above the surface, prevented them wading in.

The stately grey heron

And a chain of polystyrene floats anchored round the edge were also effective. As a result, it should now be possible to prosecute those who shoot herons, even if they can be proved to be doing damage, if the fish-farmer has not taken such reasonable means to deter them.

In Denmark, where fish farming is an important food industry, it is legally compulsory to protect fish stew-ponds by caging them in which, of course, prevents any damage at all. A fringe benefit is that the deprived herons turn their attention to eels which damage the banks of rivers and pools.

It is vastly encouraging to find an organisation like the RSPB which has teeth and is not afraid to use them, while other bodies do little but pussyfoot about in case they offend someone. In June last year, two RSPB officers paid a visit to a chap in Essex, where they found nine peregrine falcons which were said to have been bred on the premises. The officers didn't believe it and, last month, the owner was fined a record £2,000 with £500 costs, which should discourage him from having falcons taken illegally from the nest.

The RSPB prosecuted others for similar offences, with fines of several hundred pounds resulting. Sadly, a man who took a golden eagle from a nest was only reprimanded by the Inverness Sheriff's Court. But Scotland is notably backward in conservation matters and took years after the more civilised parts of Britain to ban the steel gin and otter hunting.

I trust that such minor setbacks will not deter the RSPB's good works and I only wish other organisations were half as effective.

48.   A Place For The Weeds

During the early summer, the tranquil air of sleepy villages all over the country will yowl to the evening serenade of angry lawn-mowers giving rough village greens a short-back-and-sides. The lily-white hands of commuters will blossom with blisters as they thrash brambles with bill-hooks or emulate Father Time by laying low the squitch on roadside verges with a scythe. Old ladies with trowels and children with rakes and hoes will be press-ganged into battle for supremacy in the annual tidy-village competition.

'Tidying up' the village of South Newington in Oxfordshire

In two weeks, raiding parties of judges will make surprise attacks on every village which enters the competition, tour every street and alley to look for litter and unkempt gardens, weeds and overgrown hedges, pretty gardens, and peaceful churchyards.

There's no doubt that such competitions have improved the standards of maintenance in many villages and perhaps boosted the tourist industry by giving visitors subjects to paste in their photograph albums. But perhaps some judges confuse 'neatness' with 'best kept'. A village garden is an empty shell unless there is a blackbird singing in the apple tree and house martins nesting beneath the eaves. But blackbirds like thickets to nest in and martins leave their trade mark on the ground beneath the nest. So if I were judge in a best-kept village competition, I would give bonus marks for every tenanted nest box and for every brood of fledglings the villagers could show.

Proper cottage gardens have a wide variety of scented flowers, plenty of herbs, dense hedges and thickets of shrubs. The snag is that breeding grounds for all sorts of wildlife all over the country are getting unavoidably scarcer and scarcer. Mechanisation on farms is irreversible, but because huge machines cannot cavort around in little fields, hundreds of miles of hedgerows are grubbed out annually. Every hedge that is destroyed not only makes it harder for many birds to find a building site, it also makes it easier for their enemies to find the nests they build. Little woods and copses suffer the same fate, as do the small pools when 'clean' (chlorinated) water is piped to troughs for cattle to drink.

My solution to disappearing wild places would be to manage and develop every suitable site so that gardens in a village could provide a significant area of great variety which could be superb for wildlife sanctuaries. I say 'could' because great damage is done to many such miniature paradises through sheer ignorance.

The conservation lobby, for instance, is continually battling with farmers because they insist on putting bulls in fields and spraying their crops with poisonous pesticides. The weight of public opinion is forcing the Ministry of Agriculture to withdraw some of the worst poisons from its lists. But the irony is that some of these poisons which are no longer available for agricultural use can still be bought by gardeners to kill the greenfly on their roses.

So let's not use poisons, even to scoop first prize for a tidy garden –

and let's not be as neat as the really prissy judges would like. After all, nothing is more beautiful than butterflies basking in the sun on buddleia in a cottage garden; they love this plant although many of them, such as flamboyant peacocks and red admirals, need other plants to feed their caterpillars. Such as nettles, for instance. Just the sort of 'weeds' the best-kept village judges knock off marks for. But most flowers have long periods of dull green foliage before they blossom into glory and I can't see that nettles are less beautiful than rhododendrons, azaleas or roses before they flower. A weed is simply a wild flower in the wrong place – what is right and what is wrong is simply a matter of opinion.

So I should like to start a fashion for growing not only beautiful or neat plants in the garden. There should also be room for those which, although they don't look so gorgeous, may contribute more than their share by encouraging wild birds or beautiful butterflies to breed.

If some little man from the Town Hall comes round trying to persuade country folk to convert their villages to the impersonal uniformity of lifeless city parks, let's chuck him in the nearest nettle bed!

49. The Sting In The Tale

Although I eat my own honey for breakfast every day of the year, I freely admit that I don't like bees. Nothing would induce me to get near enough to a hive of the spiteful, stinging brutes to open it with my own fair hands, so I jumped at the chance when a stranger asked if he could put some of his bees in our wood. I had visions of a spoonful of honey with my toast that would neither be paid for in hard-earned cash nor painful stings.

It worked fine for a few years until even I got a twinge of conscience and thought that the least I could do would be to buy a hive of my own and persuade the friendly beekeeper to look after some of my bees while he was doing his own.

It was then I discovered that nothing ever goes right with the noggin-headed insects – even if you are an expert beekeeper! When the flowers were in bloom, the weather was always too cold or wet for bees to work, or there was none of the right sort of flowers in the wood. Or, if there were, there were too many Queen bees, and most of the colony uprooted themselves and flew away to start a new colony of their own.

In hard winters, most of the silly creatures die off and the survivors take most of next summer to rebuild their numbers, by which time the honey season is over. In warm winters, they emerge too soon and burn themselves out before the honey is flowing. Beekeepers can't win and honey is worth ten times as much as it sells for!

Only last week, the biggest and strongest hive swarmed and, when I paused in passing to admire their boundless energy, raping acres of sweet, white clover, I got a nasty shock. They had done so badly last year that we had moved all five hives to a warm and sunny clearing where they would only have to tumble out of bed to land in clover. I never have been able to discover what happened to most of them except that their numbers diminished almost to vanishing point. It really seemed as if they had amalgamated and that the strongest colony had made a takeover bid for the rest.

Failure last year had left such a bitter taste that anything seemed

153

better than nothing and the highlight of any walk round the wood was to revel in their productivity. So, when the truth dawned that the last decent hive no longer throbbed with activity, I passed the bad tidings on to the expert, who shrugged off the fact that they had swarmed and slung their hook to found a colony somewhere else.

For all the emotion he displayed, losing 50 or 60 lbs. of honey and thousands of bees was something that happened daily. Having resigned myself to another winter when the cupboard would be pretty bare, I got that rarest of all beekeeper's delights – a pleasant surprise.

Two years ago, a naturalist friend of mine had brought me a colony of wild bumble bees in a wooden box, with a hole at the base just large enough for bumble bees to crawl through. He assured me that I should have no trouble in getting them settled and that I could spent countless happy hours studying their habits. It goes without saying that it was just another beekeeper's tall story. When I went to examine them a couple of days later, all that I was left with was an empty box.

To collect the hen eggs, I had to pass close to this old bumble bee box and I was suddenly aware of the sort of deep droning hum that enemy bombers made in wartime, and it took a while for my ears to get attuned to locate the direction. It came from the bumble bee box and it was the result of the combined chorus of thousands of honey bees, with never a shop steward bee in sight to wither their productivity!

One honey bee looks much like another to my amateur eyes, but circumstantial evidence would suggest that the colony from the 'good' hive in the wood had decided that my antique bumble bee hive was just the sort of desirable residence they had been looking for. I telephoned the expert to come and move them back, but he has accepted defeat and left them where they are.

When he looked in the box, he said they had made a honeycomb for themselves and were filling it with 'wild' honey. So he robbed their nest, cutting out some of the luscious honeycomb, which he left at the house for my breakfast. Normal honeycomb is put there by the beekeeper and left for the bees to fill, but the kind they make themselves is beyond compare. So is the honey, which has a most delicate flavour, far better than the stuff extracted from the artificial 'supers' of conventional hives. I feel we've really hit the honey jackpot this year!

50.   Seeking Safety In Flight

The fallow fawn subsided into the heart of a clump of ferns on the edge of the wood about a hundred yards from my study window. I had watched her for the last half-hour through a pair of powerful binoculars that made her look like a golden rabbit swaying on uncontrollable wobbly stilt-like legs. Foals have legs as long in proportion, but they are wholly functional because day-old foals are supposed to be able to match full-grown mares for speed. Provided they don't have to gallop too far, a herd of mares and their foals can give most predators the go-by.

The delicate sprite on the edge of our wood had no chance of doing that. She is this year's daughter of Honey, my tame fallow deer, and after the old doe had suckled at dusk, she wandered off to leave her fawn to its own devices. Although so obviously built for speed, the tiny creature had no illusions. The instant her supper was done, instinct directed her to curl up in the thicket rather than to expose herself as tempting quarry for any predator that fancied her.

She lay curled as tight as a sleeping cat, the white spots on her gingery coat merging with her background as inconspicuous as the dapples of sunlight on the woodland floor. She didn't so much as bat an eyelid when I bent down and gently moved her to ascertain whether she was a buck or a doe.

All deer naturally seek safety from their enemies in flight, except for the first few days after birth when they turn such instincts upside down. Then they cower immobile as statues, trusting the danger will go away before they are discovered. If the worst does come to the worst, their timid mother may be inspired with fleeting courage.

I was once watching a roe deer's kid hidden in rushes after feeding, when Bill Brock, my old hand-reared badger, wandered into the area where the kid lay hidden. It was a perfectly innocent approach for he was simply grubbing for juicy worms, but the kid's mother took no chances. The instant she realised the badger was set on a course that would bring him within smelling distance of her precious kid, she

155

Fallow deer escaping into the haven of woodland

erupted with the ferocity of a bolt from a crossbow. Rocketing at full speed over the unsuspecting brock, she clouted him viciously with her chisel-sharp front hooves. The poor chap didn't know what had hit him. What's more he didn't stop to find out, but bolted for home.

Honey didn't attack me when I approached her fawn, partly perhaps because I reared her on the bottle years ago and we have established mutual trust.* But deer deem discretion the better part of valour where men are concerned. Well-meaning do-gooders, stumbling across very young fawns, at this time of year, often pick them up in the belief that they have been 'deserted' by their mother. If they taint them with the pong of humans, the chances are that they *will* be deserted, though the does would otherwise have returned to suckle them if nobody had meddled.

* *see Country Seasons*, page 112

156

Now that the main crop of fawns are about three weeks old, the whole herd has reverted to the familiar pattern of seeking safety in flight. Not only do the youngsters rush madly away if they are disturbed, but they spend long hours practising the art of evasion.

Play in all young animals is not for amusement but for a deadly serious purpose. Kittens chasing ping-pong balls are practising catching prey, and puppies' mock fights are to teach them to hunt in a pack. Our fallow fawns play endless games of tag. One will rush off and the others follow in wild break-neck dashes through the thickets of the wood. They learn every snag and obstacle so that they can weave through hazards that would defeat strangers in pursuit. Although their antics leave us spellbound by their grace and speed, such play has the serious purpose of teaching them the techniques of survival.

51.   Youth Out-twitches The Twitchers

Twitching is a symptom of rather nasty nervous disorders, but Twitchers – or Twits for short – is the name given to a sub-species of the common Bird Watcher, *Ornithologist vulgaris*. These Twitchers, though fortunately fairly rare, are often seen on the banks of reservoirs, in deep woodland, open moorland or any habitat where someone has been rash enough to report the presence of a rare bird.

Twits can often be recognised by their plumage, which has usually been purchased from Government surplus stores where it has apparently mouldered for a long time. Woollen hats, khaki or camouflage anoraks, huge boots and woollen socks are usually worn by both sexes, which appear identical to superficial examination. Bushy beards give some clue that the wearer may be male, though this is by no means infallible.

The sad thing is that these Twitchers get respectable bird watchers a bad name. They are not naturalists but simply collectors of the names of species of bird that they claim to have observed. In the Twits' kindergarten, they start off with a complete list of all resident British birds and they spend their spare time travelling round, ticking off the name of each bird that they see. A wet Sunday on the banks of a reservoir could add the names of common ducks and geese and other waterfowl.

All very harmless and healthy you might think and up to this stage it is. But the more ticks they get on their lists, the harder it grows to see the rarities they have missed. And, if they *have* logged all the British birds, there are always the rarities blown in on storms from foreign lands.

This is where the Twits make a nuisance of themselves. A river warbler was recently reported on farmland in Norfolk and the Twitchers unfortunately got wind of it. River warblers are not found in Britain and most bird books do not even include them in the index. They are undistinguished little brown birds with a song that, I am told,

'So that's what you look like!'

is more of a metallic jingle than a trill. But they are so rare that they have never been reported in England until the recent arrival in Norfolk. A river warbler on a Twitcher's list would be a status symbol better than an enemy chieftain's scalp to a Red Indian.

Twitchers turned up from far and wide, accidentally put on the scent by the report of a local birdwatcher. There was a public footpath through the field where the bird had settled, but that meant nothing to them. They trampled a field of growing rye to get a better look, setting up their binoculars and telescopes where they could see best, without giving a damn for the farmer's crops. Respectable bird watchers cannot be surprised that they are not welcomed with open arms by landowners when such silly minorities get their hobby such a bad name.

My only experience with feathered rarities was a few years ago within three miles of the centre of Birmingham. The Natural History Society of a local school has permission to visit land between the Bristol Road and the University. It is an astonishingly peaceful and secluded spot – except for the constant rumble of traffic down the Bristol Road.

A fifteen-year-old boy, whom I discovered to be a first-rate naturalist, heard bird song there that he couldn't identify and hours of patient waiting eventually disclosed a little brown bird that he had never seen before. This eventually turned out to be a Cetti's warbler – another 'little brown job', not unlike the bird that enticed the Twitchers into the rye. A very experienced ornithologist eventually identified it and I was asked to talk to the finder about it for the BBC natural history programme 'Living World'. The producer wanted to encourage the young naturalist but to keep the location strictly secret to avoid an invasion of Twits which could have jeopardised the chances of the school to continue to use the site for the keen youngsters in the Natural History Society.

We had to get up at five in the morning to make a recording of the Cetti's warbler's song, to prove that it was there! Once the real traffic started down the Bristol Road, there was no chance of a decent recording.

It so happened that, although Cetti's warblers have been reported in this country several times since then, my young friend had discovered one of the first two specimens recorded. It would have been irresistible to Twitchers – so the producer did not include the item in a programme until the bird had safely gone.

What I enjoyed most was the young naturalist's attitude. Rarity meant nothing to him. He was simply interested in the hows and whys of the bird's arrival. Real naturalists enjoy common creatures as much as exotic rarities. When a rarity does cross their path, it is the problems of integrating with our native animals and birds which are exciting. Ticking off names on a list is no more rewarding than the acquisitive greed of any other form of collectors' mania. No wonder they call them Twitchers.

160

52. Rarity For Rarity's Sake

There has never been more needle between farmers and conservationists. The Wildlife and Countryside Bill tottered uncertainly through Parliament and sparked off differences that have smouldered for years.

The question of SSSIs headed the list of flashpoints. (SSSI is the bureaucratic jargon for a Site of Special Scientific Interest.) The title can be slapped on a boggy meadow where wild flowers that need wet conditions flourish. The meadow at the top end of our wood, where the wild daffodils grow, has been classed with this highfalutin title. A moor that grows rare mosses or where scarce birds nest can be classed by the Nature Conservancy Council as an SSSI and so can ancient woodland or water meadow.

All too often, the criterion for designation is simply the cult of rarity. An obscure spider or lichen or insect is all that is necessary to have the site where it breeds or survives labelled for posterity – whether the owner likes it or not.

Therein lies the snag. At present, the designation means very little because there is no law to prevent the owner of a boggy meadow draining it to grow more crops, or getting a licence to fell an ancient wood and to replace it by fast-growing soft woods. One of the original objects of the Wildlife and Countryside Bill was to make it illegal for an owner to alter the status of an SSSI without the same sort of planning permission that would be required to change the appearance of a listed house. It failed and can only delay change of use for a year, for which compensation may be awarded.

The Bill seeks to do many other things, from banning the cruel type of snares used by the Ministry of Agriculture to catch badgers, to controlling farming practices on moorland. It is so indigestible that eager-beavers, pulling all directions, look like getting nowhere.

To my mind, the sponsors of the bill made two fundamental errors. They laid too much emphasis on the cult of rarity, for rarity's sake, and they refused to admit that it is impossible to stop the clock and freeze time in its paces. As climate gradually alters and farming methods change, there have always been some creatures which thrive better than ever before and some that can't stand the pace. Many common butterflies are now scarce because they have been wiped out by poisonous pesticides or their food plants have been 'controlled' by weed killers.

It seems sensible to put pressure on manufacturers to produce fewer dangerous but more selective chemicals to try to preserve whole ranges of harmless species that are, at present, wiped out with the pests. This would surely be more practical than tilting at windmills by trying to stop the clock to save some obscurity at the expense of alienating farmers trying to wrest a living from the land where it survives.

The Woodland Trust is having a drive this autumn (1981) to persuade people to replace some of the hardwood trees that have been recently felled. More oaks, ash, beech and other native trees have been felled in the last forty years than in the previous four hundred. So people will be invited to contribute £1 to plant a tree or considerably more to have a small wood dedicated to their memory.

All very laudable and few would quarrel with it. However, instead of marshalling the sympathies of those who own the land where the trees will be planted, the Woodland Trust leaflets alienate them.

Announcing the scheme, the foreword sounds off about 'scandals' and 'wanton destruction', saying that woods have 'vanished under prairies of plough' or been replaced by 'palls of conifers' which have buried spring flowers and medieval earthworks alike. It doesn't say that, four centuries ago when the land was far more densely wooded, the population was a tenth of the present size. Nor does it say that a high proportion of our national woodland was felled from dire necessity in two world wars.

There is almost equal pressure on moorland farmers who try to convert acres of sterility into fertile land that can produce food. Conservationists scream about 'spoiling the view'. They overlook the fact that the greatest danger to humanity is the population explosion and that, if we don't learn to grow more food, war or pestilence will surely cut us down to size. Their rose-tinted specs refuse to focus on the fact that the modern earth-moving machinery, developed in two world wars, now makes it possible to cultivate land such as moorland. And they conveniently forget that our ancestors cleared the scrub from the open moorland in generations gone by. It wasn't always moorland!

The fact is that the countryside never stands still. People who live in towns and treat the country as their playground, seem oblivious of the fact that most farmers and landowners, who have their roots in the land, love it at least as dearly as any starry-eyed romantic. They have to, or they wouldn't put up with the hardships of storm and drought to wrest a living from the land.

53. Home Sweet Home-Cured Is Best

Any Black Countryman of my generation will tell you that there is no picture upon his wall to equal a side of home-cured bacon and a haunch of home-cured ham. In both world wars, we had a 'house pig' which we fed on whatever scraps we could scrounge, whatever spuds we could grow and an inadequate ration of 'utility' mash which the government allocated if we let them have half the pig to swell the national larder. In the last war, we got rations for two pigs and so were allowed to keep a whole one for ourselves.

In my teens Old Ebenezer Atkins, skilled in the secret arts of true countrymen, taught me to dry-salt ham and bacon. Twenty-four hours after the pig was killed, when its hairs had been scrubbed off its hide with scalding water, a side of bacon was laid on the slab to be salted. Rough salt was then rubbed in until the surface began to lather and the skin on the palms of my hands achieved a leathery consistency in sheer self-defence. The salt got into any cracks or minute cuts until tales of salt being rubbed into the weals on the backs of criminals caused by the cat o' nine tails made my own flesh creep.

Just when the agony was more than I could bear, old Ebenezer would produce the second side, and get me going on that. To add injury to insult, we had to salt the hams as soon as we had done the sides. Then we put them on a bed of salt in a slate trough, put a pinch of saltpetre round the ham bones, and left them to 'soak' for a couple of days. We turned them and kept them nicely covered till Ebenezer reckoned the salt had gone into the soul of the meat.

For the last few days, we added crystals of brown sugar to sweeten the hams. This was theoretically impossible to get during the war, but it was astonishing what grocers could produce – for a few slices of home-cured ham to fry with an egg on Sunday morning.

The bacon was ready to be washed free of external salt in about ten days and the ham in three weeks. Sides and hams were then hung in an

This piglet is certainly free-range

airy kitchen to dry before being fitted in muslin bags, to keep the flies off until we were ready to eat them.

No ham ever tasted sweeter and no bacon more luscious. A couple of slices of either, crowned by golden-yolked eggs and reposing on crisp fried bread, cooked in the ham's own generous fat, was a banquet fit for a king.

We gave up keeping pigs for a time after the war because it is so easy to grow idle when your belly doesn't pinch. I had intermittent goes at keeping them in the wood, not so much for the food they supply as for the good they do the trees.

It isn't generally realised how much the finest native hard woods owe to pigs. In days gone by, commoners had the right of 'pannage', which allowed them to run a few pigs in their local wood or forest to mop up the surplus acorns in the autumn. Acorns, in excess, are poisonous to cattle so the pigs saved casualties and fed well on the natural food themselves. They also planted oak trees for future generations by treading a few they didn't find just the right depth into the ground to germinate and sprout.

So I put pigs in my wood where I wanted thickets to replace patches of bracken – and the spin-off reminded me of the superb home-cured hams of my boyhood. Our free-range pigs were even better than the home-fed pigs, kept in sties, just as free-range eggs are superior to anything that factory farms produce. The only snag was that we had to supplement their natural food with corn and carry water up the wood so that the prospect of the work involved has lately put us off.

A recent news item* threatens to change my mind again. Officials of the Ministry of Agriculture, Fisheries and Food have been bombarded with complaints that modern ham and bacon is unacceptably mushy. Hung as a picture on the wall, a modern side of bacon would be worse than rising damp. Forced by public opinion to investigate, they have discovered that some shop ham contains over twenty-three per cent curing solution or water. Some commercial curers have discovered that the addition of polyphosphates increase the water-retaining properties of meat until almost a quarter, by weight, is pure water.

The same effect can be achieved by the mechanical tumbling tech-

* This was originally written in August 1981

166

niques employed by the latest meat-curing machinery. One firm, wishing to instal the most sophisticated equipment available, advertised its obsolete plant in trade papers under the tempting heading, 'Why sell meat when you can sell water?'

Even bureaucracy could not be seen to turn a blind eye to that. The Ministry of Agriculture took dynamic action. It produced a set of rules designed to stamp out the sharp practice. It is not going to allow ham to be sold as 'ham' if it contains more than ten per cent of water. If it contains more than ten per cent of water or curing solution, there must be a label to say so! And if it contains more than twenty-three percent, it cannot be sold as 'ham' at all. It must be called 'processed ham'.

So, if you relish being rooked a pound or so for a pound of water, just look for the label 'processed ham'. Oh, for the days of a pig in the sty!

Bureaucrats are not notable for tearing themselves apart with effort, though. I have to warn you that, by the time the Ministry regulations come into force, you will probably have forgotten my warning about paying through the nose for the water in processed ham. It is not unreasonable to expect that, having uncovered such a monumental fiddle and devised regulations (however inadequate) to curb it, that they would put them in force pretty smartly.

Not so. The Ministry's grandiose plan does not take effect until – wait for it – July 1983. Two solid years' delay. Why? Has someone received a rich backhander not to spoil the wide boys' fun, or is there some legitimate reason that has escaped me?

Perhaps the Men from the Ministry will tell us?

54. Chase-me Charlies

I am often asked if foxes kill cats, and the plain fact is that I don't know. I do know that they will eat rabbits, pheasants and poultry because I have witnessed the hunt and the kill, and frequently seen the evidence. A temporary shortage of eggs is due to the fact that a fox killed five of my laying hens in the wood a few weeks ago, though that particular fox will not offend again.

Most gamekeepers will tell you that foxes certainly kill cats – but so do gamekeepers! And if they can persuade fond owners of missing pussies to blame old Charlie Fox, it bends the finger of suspicion away from them. So keepers' accusations are not exactly disinterested.

A recent letter I received from a reader is at least unbiased and gives an eye-witness account of what appears to be a serious cat hunt, with Charlie replacing the hounds. Or was it innocent play? The correspondent had been watching a programme on television about town foxes and he was surprised to hear the statement that foxes and cats 'tolerated' each other. He said that when in a friend's house in his neighbourhood, a cat 'came tearing across the lawn with a fox after it. They vanished into a shrubbery and, seconds later, the cat came out, with the fox still after it, into another shrubbery.' The letter went on to say: 'The fox had not got a bushy tail, so would it have been a young one?'

If it was a cub, I suppose the possibility is that they were only playing. And, even if the fox was adult, it is reasonable to assume that a fox could catch a cat on the ground if it really wanted to and a cat could climb a tree, if it was really scared. The tail is not much of a clue because an adult fox could be moulting into a new coat at this time of year, so could have a mangy-looking brush. Town foxes are often mangy in any case, and a hungry, mangy adult could easily catch a cat.

But foxes are no fools and cats are tough customers. So even if this fox was not playing, it is quite possible that it chickened out in preference to getting an eye scratched as the price of a tasty dinner. There's not much doubt that cat would come fairly high as a gastronomic delicacy on

The fox never caught the geese although they were threatened at night

foxes' menus because keepers often use dead cats as bait, to be laced with poison, when thinning out the foxes in their pheasant coverts. It is, of course, illegal to lay poison in the open, but what goes on in secluded corners of a keeper's beat has always been difficult to prove. And cat, as bait, has always been considered irresistible to foxes.

My own guess is that a hungry fox would catch and eat a kitten or weakly cat with as little compunction as it would have in tackling a rabbit. But I very much doubt if any fox in his right mind would risk the spitting, scratching fury of a really frightened adult cat. Nor do I think that adult foxes and cats would indulge in the sort of rough play that was described.

Our play is for exercise or to amuse ourselves. Animals' play is serious practice for the business of survival. Hunting animals, such as dogs, seems to enjoy mock battles to get them in trim to defend their territory, or chases to train them to catch the prey they hunt.

The creatures they prey on practise escape routines. Deer dash through thickets where pursuers, who didn't know the exact lie of the land, would pile up in pursuit.

It isn't very common to see play between animals of different species except under the artificial conditions of domestic animals. I should need a lot of convincing that any sensible cat would play chase-me-Charlie with a fox who had never been introduced to her. But I often get letters from readers who have seen similar occurrences.

What worries me most is the possibility that rabies, the killer disease already just across the English Channel, should ever be brought into this country. It wouldn't matter then whether the fox and cat were playing or whether the drama was in deadly earnest.

If a fox were scratched or bitten by a rabid dog or cat which had been smuggled into the country, it would contract the disease. The spread would then be impossible to control because the fox would bite almost any living creature within reach and, having become such a common urban species, town foxes would inevitably infect domestic dogs and cats. The statement in the film that was shown on television went on to say that town foxes are harmless creatures. They may be harmless now, but if ever rabies does come, town foxes will be as dangerous as unexploded bombs. Injections against the disease are the fiendishly painful alternative to agonising death and, even then, the injections are by no means a certain cure or prevention.

So I should feel a lot safer if there were far fewer town foxes than there are, not for the sake of night-prowling cats, but to limit the risks to their owners. The fact is that foxes are now commoner in many towns than they are in the country, because the loss of laying hens or lambs or pheasants gets rural trigger fingers uncommonly itchy so that the cheeky Charlies get short shrift.

55. Ticker-tape Clue And My Badgers Are Back

Within a hundred yards of my study window a hole as big as your head has been scooped out of the turf. It is a neat basin in the soil, obviously excavated by a craftsman, but the clinical effect is marred by an untidy litter of a brittle, papery substance. It looks as if some solicitor's clerk had been shredding ancient legal documents into parchment ticker-tape.

I was delighted to see the evidence for two reasons. Close inspection disclosed twenty or thirty wood wasps lying dead in the litter, which is

Young badgers outside their sett

all that is left of their nest, so they won't crawl into my beer mug. And the fact that the nest has been dug out is clear proof that badgers are once more active in my wood. My neighbour now employs an extremely co-operative keeper and I believe it to be no coincidence that the wood has been recolonised by badgers since the arrival of a helpful keeper over my boundary.

Autumn, the generous season of ripe fruit, also produced the wasps to share it with us. And, just as the wasps regard the fruit as their crop, badgers take a harvest from the wasp grubs, which they lay bare by digging out the wasp nests. There is not the least shadow of doubt about this and any countryman can tell you about the mutilated wasp nests he has found after the badgers have ravaged them. The strange thing is that I don't know anyone who can describe, in an eye-witness account, exactly how the badgers do it!

I have watched badgers for more than forty years. I kept a tame badger, which I hand-reared, for ten years* and had hand-reared badgers living in a sett near the house, but as free as the air to go where they liked in the wood or on adjacent farms. I have seen literally scores of wasp nests after badgers had dug them out, broken them up and consumed the luscious maggots which would otherwise have grown into wasps. But I don't know how they do it!

In order to find out, I once took Bill Brock, my tame boar badger, to a bank where wasps had their nest and waited to see what he did. He was rooting about, looking for earthworms or the big, fat, juicy slugs which badgers love so much. Suddenly he stopped in his tracks, one forefoot raised as a dog will do when it is puzzled. He cocked his head on one side, obviously listening, and then slowly and deliberately, he approached the hole in the bank where the wasp nest was. I am quite convinced that he located that nest, not by the smell but by the sound of wasp wings, droning their menacing war cry a few inches under the soil.

Bill Brock took two or three strides towards the nest, until his short-sighted, piggy little eyes located the entrance hole. Then he stuffed his leathery snout down it and inhaled an exhilarating aroma of those succulent grubs. Now I would see what others didn't know, now I had cracked it. Or so I thought!

---

* *see Badgers at My Window*

173

He started to dig furiously, broke through the crust of the nest and the inmates exploded in a cloud. But he discovered that the chasm he had exposed was as full of pain as any cavity opened by dentists in a hollow tooth. Excited badgers fluff out their fur as straight as the fluebrush of an angry cat's tail – and Bill puffed out to twice his size.

Boffins say that badgers can excavate wasp nests with impunity because the insects find it impossible to shove through this tangle of erect hairs near enough to the skin for their stings to penetrate. This may be 90% true, but boffins in laboratories can't see what was obvious to me. Poor Bill had no long hairs to puff out round his lips and his sensitive tongue was utterly naked! He shook his head, first in anger and then in desperation to escape – and immediately decided that there were better things to do in life than to get badly stung for the sake of a few lousy wasp grubs.

I was no nearer to unravelling the secret of how they dig out nests but suffer so little damage that they are fit enough to enjoy the spoils, so I repeated the experiment with a bumble bee nest – with the same lack of success.

Don't run away with the idea that my badger was a bit of a pansy because the fact was that he was a very tough guy indeed and fought horrific battles with wild badgers in the wood to establish a territory for himself.

My own theory is that wasps are far quieter during the hours of darkness than by daylight so that it would be easier to scrape the earth covering of a nest away, very quietly and very slowly, without alerting the wasps. In the chill air before dawn, they would also be sluggish and less aggressive than when I introduced Bill Brock. But, like other countrymen, I still have no proof. It is still one of the secrets that Nature keeps up her sleeve!

56.   Ride Him, Cowboy!

At about the age of eight, I was taken for a holiday to Burton Bradstock in Dorset, where we stayed on a farm. The fields ran down to the sea, which I saw only once in the fortnight we were there because I was far more interested in what went on at the farm.

It was about September but, in those days, stubble was not burned or ploughed straight in. Poultry was taken out to glean the golden fallen grain and, at dawn and dusk, shimmering pheasants came out to join them.

The farmer on 'our farm' had bigger ideas. He turned out a herd of pigs to root and feed, and he sent his youngest son, as honorary pig-herd, to see that they did not stray on to adjacent crops that were yet to be harvested.

I was about the same age as young Tommy and, to my great delight, I was invited to join him as the pig-herd's assistant. My boss, the chief honorary pig-herd, was an artist at the job and he initiated me into the mysteries of making a quick assessment of the pecking order of the herd.

Pigs are very like us in that there are definite boss pigs and lower orders of porcine society who follow the boss pig's lead as gullibly as any human mob. And, in common with modern mobs, our herd of pigs seemed hell-bent on destruction. One minute 'our' leader, an old brown sow which had obviously suckled a lifetime of litters, was stretched out as comfortably abandoned as an old lady sunning herself on a crowded beach. The next, she was in full gallop towards the field of turnips the other side of a straggly hedge, with the herd in close order behind her.

Tommy was almost psychic at reading the boss pig's mind. I never discovered how he did it, but he seemed to know a split second before the sow herself made up her mind precisely when she would make a bolt for it and in which direction.

Tommy was obviously executive material. As his assistant, I was expected to run faster than the pigs to plug whatever gap in the hedge Tommy had deduced the old sow was intent on breaching. Inexperienced folk, who have never had a race with a pig, can have no conception of just how fast they can run. I was no slouch at the age of eight, but if my charges got anything of a start on me there was little chance of my heading them off. If I got there first, the old sow, as all good leaders do, respected my superiority, wheeled round and resumed rooting up the stubble.

The worst of all worlds was when she gained a lead, not only on me but on her followers. She would then dive through the gap with the speed and agility of a rugby three-quarter, leaving me to turn and face the charging mob and try to stop them in their tracks. A child of eight trying to prevent a herd of pigs following their leader had about as much chance of success as Canute had of stopping the waves. They surged each side of me until the inevitable happened and one of them knocked my feet from under me. Then the rest surged over me, their sharp little cloven hooves pummelling my ribs to encourage me to run faster next time.

I persuaded Tommy that we would stand a better chance of success if each took a separate side of the field, taking care of one end hedge and one side apiece. That meant that if they went his way, it would be his job, not mine, to head them off, which halved my risks. As I also managed to pick the side where there were no attractive crops, leaving the turnip side to him, I reckon I should have qualified as honorary pig-herd with Tommy as my honorary assistant if I had returned next year!

He had a skill, though, that I envied, but never had the courage to emulate. He used to ride the bull! Tommy's dad had a herd of cows which earned their living by producing meat or milk and it was important to get them in calf a few weeks after they had calved last time, so that they calved at about yearly intervals.

When cows are out in the fields, it isn't immediately obvious to human eyes precisely when they are in season and ready to be mated. Bulls, however, have no difficulty in deciding the time, so the obvious thing is to run a loose bull with the herd so that he can bull them as soon as they are ready.

Tommy's dad kept Jason, an enormous Hereford bull, permanently running with the cows. Jason must have weighed about a ton, but this mountain of beef on the hoof was about as amiable as any paunchy old sugar daddy. When Tommy was sent to bring in the cows, he only half opened the gate so that they had to come out in single file. By perching on the gate post, he could drop on to Jason's back as he passed and the huge beast took less notice of him than he would have done of a fly. They headed the herd all down the village street, scattering visitors who didn't know how quiet he was, while I brought up the rear goading the sluggards.

But much as I envied him his apparently perilous ride, cow-herd was the one department where I was content to remain honorary assistant.

57.   Whose Countryside Is It, Anyway?

The planners are playing the fool with the countryside again. This time it is with redundant farm buildings. The modern trend of replacing farm labour with machines has resulted in bigger and bigger machines which can't manoeuvre in little fields. The most obvious result of this is that hundreds of miles of hedgerow are grubbed out annually, turning the patchwork of little, odd-shaped fields into featureless prairies of plough.

Conservationists are always bellyaching about this because they say it spoils the view. Naturalists bemoan the fact that there is less food and cover to encourage breeding birds. A less obvious effect is that the new mammoth machines are far too big to cram into traditional farm buildings, designed generations ago when horses were the motive power.

In those days, cattle were tethered in stalls and milked by hand, which resulted in cow sheds that were long, low, warm and cosy. Among my most pleasant childhood memories is the sweet scent of contented cattle and the slow rhythm of endless cud being chewed.

Cattle are now kept in huge concrete yards and milked mechanically in cow parlours, where one man can manage a hundred cows instead of a fifth of the number. So cow sheds have joined stables and cart sheds in the catalogue of useless buildings. The harsh fact is that picturesque and ancient farmsteads are often useless to modern farmers because they need far too much labour to man them.

All over the country, I see derelict farm buildings which have been replaced by ultra-modern concrete and asbestos. However attractive disused buildings may look in the distance, they look pretty crummy at close quarters when the roofs are sagging and the whole place is wrapped in a blanket of nettles.

Some farmers knock them down, with or without planning permission, although there is an increasing tendency to apply for planning permission to change their traditional use. The most popular alternative is to convert them into houses – either holiday homes or for

178

Cyril West milks his cows the old-fashioned way: Upware in Cambridgeshire

permanent use. In areas like the Peak National Park, in Derbyshire, the authorities have been pretty sensible.

Small farms are often not viable, so it is common to find several small farms merged with all the buildings at headquarters, leaving several houses and farmsteads empty. Many of these have been converted to flatlets or houses, often managed as a 'cash crop' by the farmer. This fits in with the concept of a national park, because it enables extra visitors to recharge their energies in wide open spaces without destroying the peaceful views with huts, caravans and all the unsightly trash that too often mars the countryside.

But most of the countryside does not consist of national parks. It consists of pleasant little villages within commuting reach of the large towns where so many people have to go for jobs. Life in these villages

179

has altered immensely since the war. Farm workers are paid far more than they were and many of them no longer wish to live in the isolated cottages where generations of their ancestors lived. They have moved to council estates in the village and their houses are now occupied by city folk whose main ambition has been to 'get away from it all'. Most of these incomers to villages are highly-paid executive types, well used to the hurly-burly of modern life.

Having bought a country cottage for a big price and spent as much or more again on modernising it, they have no intention of seeing their investment wither and shrink. Some are far more jealous of further change than the greyest grey beard among the native inhabitants. So they jostle the locals out of the way to take the key positions on the local council, Women's Institute and garden guild. Before they know where they are, the natives have been displaced by a new ruling class who decide how the village shall be run. Most old villages now have 'Conservation Areas' where nobody may alter the outside of his cottage without planning approval granted by officials influenced by committees of incomers protecting their investments.

Fine, in theory. But all too often the Conservation Areas are mere shells, running along the village street. Out of sight behind the street is a modern development of unimaginative little boxes, flogged off by some speculative builder with an eye to the main chance and a seat on the council.

When too many newcomers arrive, they alter the whole personality of a village so that the countryside is governed by people with urban minds, who would not know a bull from a bulrush. 'Proper' village pubs are tarted up into gin-bars, with chromium plate instead of brass and one-armed bandits and the sickly background whimper of piped music. Churches are floodlit, gravestones which commemorate generations past are ripped out by tiny men with tiny minds in the cause of tidiness.

There are bridge clubs and squash courts, everyone is for hockey and some, so they say, are not above a bit of trendy wife-swapping. On one hand, it's a swinging crowd which adds a new character (of a sort) to the countryside. But the same crowd objects to farmers who try to keep abreast of the latest techniques (which require large fields) or wish to use old buildings, which are obsolete for stock, to house a human crop to help to make ends meet.

58.   Autumn Harvest

It's been a good corn harvest in my neck of the woods. Farmers grumble a bit, they always do, but I don't see many of them riding around on push bikes!

When I was a kid, a ton of corn to the acre was reckoned to be very good. Nowadays, plenty of farmers get more than three times as much. Even the dog-and-stick brigade, who haven't caught up with modern methods, go into orbit if they get less than a couple of tons to the acre.

Now that the conventional harvest is over, the natural harvest of wild, uncultivated fruits is in full swing. Sloes, the bitter bellyaching fruit of the blackthorn, have been in rather short supply. The bushes were shimmering with white, early blossom in spring, but a few frosts put paid to the chances of much setting into fruit.

There was just one sheltered clump near the pool in Primrose Dell that bore a nice crop of berries about half the size of good black grapes. So the other evening my wife and I gathered a pound of the fruit, pierced each berry with a darning needle to make the juice run, added a pound of sugar and a bottle of gin, and put it by the pantry door. It is vital to put the jar in an inconvenient position that makes it necessary to move it at least once every day. Whoever moves it is honour-bound to shake it up so that in three or four weeks the sugar will have worked on the sloes and the sloes will have decanted their juice into the gin, which will assume a hue the colour of vintage port wine. By Christmas, it will be a liqueur fit for the gods, and makes the traditional climax to our turkey and plum pudding as we settle to hear the Queen's annual message to the nation.

Some of the harvest in the wood is just as sought after – but not by us. Acorns come top of the list. Squirrels, rooks and wood pigeons travel miles to raid the tree tops. A fringe benefit is that literally tons of them get knocked off and fall to the ground uneaten. So pheasants assemble from all over the district to feed on the bounty detached by the tree rats.

So do the fallow deer and, while I have been writing this, a party of half a dozen does have been wandering about under the oak trees in

A dormouse feeding on a hazelnut

front of my study window, stooping to gather fallen acorns every few steps. However, a surfeit of acorns can be rather poisonous to some species so pigs, exercising the right of pannage* and, at the same time, clearing up the surplus acorns, remove the risk of poisoning other stock while laying on flesh which is as superior to the insipid intensively-fed mush as free-range eggs are to a pallid tack from battery hens.

Most people know that the leaves and berries of yew trees are deadly poisonous and should be avoided at all costs. It is not uncommon for cattle, which have strayed into a wood containing yew trees, to die with the uneaten herbage in their mouths before they have even had time to swallow it. Yet deer seem to eat yew with impunity. In the New Forest, they are said to be so addicted that they stand on their hind legs and browse the yew trees as high as they can reach. Since this is higher than ponies and cattle can reach, the browsing deer put temptation out of reach of more vulnerable animals.

I once told this to a very distinguished vet, who frankly did not believe me. I had a lovely tame roe deer at the time who was as greedy as she was beautiful. So I went into the garden, picked a bunch of yew leaves and offered them to her. She wolfed them down and the vet nearly had apoplexy expecting the deer to throw a fit and die.

One man's meat is another's poison!

* *see* No. 53

59. Vigil On The Moors

I take my hat off to the Dartmoor Badger Protection League. They have the courage of their convictions. For fifty-six days – and nights – they kept vigil over a badger sett on Corndon Tor on Dartmoor, to prevent the Ministry of Agriculture rat-catchers from gassing badgers whose ancestors have lived there for centuries.

By keeping vigil, I do not mean that they propped up the bar of the local pub, waiting for gossip. They actually camped out on the moor in all the rough weather we'd been having. They had the landlord's permission, so no one could turn them off – and the Men from the Ministry would have risked legal action if they had put them in danger by spewing out their foul cyanide gas while they were there. You have got to have strong convictions of being in the right to take such drastic action, but the Ministry case for gassing is only founded on sand.

It is widely known that badgers and cattle are fellow victims of bovine TB in very localised parts of the West Country – and so are foxes and moles and rats and other animals. Nobody has been able to prove that badgers spread it, except in the highly unnatural conditions deliberately staged by scientists in the laboratory.*

But Ministry officials have got the bee in their bonnets that badgers are the culprits and they have used over seven *tons* of the obscene poisonous cyanide to try to exterminate the badger in infected areas. This has just backfired on them in a big way because it has been suggested that the poison they use liberates free cyanide, polluting the surroundings.

A farmer, living downhill from the sett they wanted to gas, demanded an assurance from the Ministry that the operation would not pollute his water. So the Ministry officials wrote saying that when gassing was undertaken, they would provide a bowser supply of water for domestic use and for livestock. They also promised to get the South-West Water Authority to test the supply for contamination, immediately before

* *see No Badgers in My Wood*

184

gassing and at least twice, at 24-hour intervals, afterwards. They gave the written assurance that they would not withdraw the bowser supply until the tests had shown the water to be safe.

That arrangement was later altered verbally, and it was said that the Ministry officials proposed to tap a water main about a quarter of a mile away (at taxpayers' expense!) to provide a piped supply while their foul work was done.

A young badger beside its sett on Dartmoor

The farmer pointed out that as the cattle live out, there was a natural supply in all fields – and there was not the slightest hope of preventing them from drinking from it. What a truly disgraceful state of affairs in a civilised country!

The Ministry officials would not convict themselves of polluting the countryside with cyanide by admitting that an alternative water supply was necessary while their rat-catchers were gassing badgers in the area unless the danger was real. So the implication is that in previous operations some of the seven tons of cyanide they have used *could*, and perhaps has, put stock or even people at risk. All because they are hell bent on exterminating badgers on purely circumstantial evidence!

The explanation for condemning the badgers is that some of them are suffering from TB, which is indisputable, and they allege that badger dung and bedding can harbour the germs for up to five months. So they claim that even when they have gassed a sett, healthy badgers which come to recolonise it months later, may be infected. When cattle are found to be infected, or when there is a reaction to the tests, they are slaughtered. Yet the cow dung and bedding on the farm is still put into a mechanical manure spreader and broadcast over the fields.

The Russians, who have done research on this, have discovered that grass contaminated by TB can prove fatal to guinea pigs up to a year later. What obscene hypocrisy, therefore, to kill badgers but spread the infection from diseased cattle on the same fields!

In Devon where the abuse is worst, public feeling is so high that 10,000 people have joined the Dartmoor Badger Protection League and it was through pressure they applied that the Government was forced to halt operations while Lord Zuckerman conducted an enquiry. Although he had been a respected scientist in his day, he is now an old man and his report was widely regarded as a purely cosmetic whitewash operation, and he recommended the gassing continue.

On the Ministry's own figures, however, out of 1,099 cases of TB, they ascribed 331 to badgers, 175 to cattle imported from Ireland, and no fewer than 446 were 'unknown'. For several months, many cattle had got into the country without proper checks. So it is not unreasonable to suspect that the total due to imported cattle could have been the major cause!

The whole affair has got completely out of control, and much would never have come to light without the dedication of the Dartmoor Badger Protection League which is ruthlessly determined to see that badgers are not used for ever as Ministry scapegoats. Members of the League have achieved partial success simply by making their feelings known to their MPs. More power to their elbows. If everyone who shares their sentiments writes to his own MP, it may still not be too late to apply enough pressure to force the Ministry to its senses.

NOTE: See author's note on page 135.

60. Lady Of The Stream

There are supposed to be more fishermen than football fans but most of them are coarse fishermen and Dora wouldn't know them.

Don't get me wrong. I'm not suggesting that chaps who line canal banks, motionless as herons, dangling maggots from their rods, are coarse. The adjective applies only to the fish they catch. Game fishermen, on the other hand, fish for the aristocrats of the piscatorial world, which include salmon and trout. They scorn the use of worms and blow fly maggots and the purists among them use artificial flies as bait. These flies are bits of feather and other material, cunningly tied to the butts of fish hooks to deceive the fish that the morsels floating on the surface will taste as appetising as they look.

Dora Oliver, guardian of the River Dove

When skilled hands have fashioned such flies to perfection, even greater skill is needed to grass a luscious trout. The fisherman creeps along the banks, looking for the concentric circles in the water that denote a trout is feeding. When a real fly is stupid enough to land on the surface, the fish edges up on him from the deep and literally sucks him down, leaving the tell-tale rounded ripples to mark the spot where the luckless fly met its fate.

The observant game fisherman opens his tackle box and selects an identikit image of the deceased insect and ties it to his fishing line so that the deadly barbed hook is cunningly concealed. He then oscillates his rod to cast the fly exactly over the snout of the feeding fish. It is a very skilled pursuit, a contest of wits and dexterity between the fisherman and his game quarry. There is nothing coarse about it! Such game fishermen, or the elite among them, number themselves as Dora Oliver's clients.

Dora is the water bailiff of several miles on the River Dove, which separates Staffordshire from Derbyshire. It is one of the most famous trout rivers in England and Dora's beat is through Berresford Dale, the most famous stretch of the Dove. It was here that the immortal Isaac Walton, who wrote the *Compleat Angler*, used to fish. To fish the Walton beat of the Dove is the ambition of all true practitioners of the art.

Rivers of such quality need specialist skills to yield the highest quality of sport. The banks have to be scythed so that sportsmen do not fall over their feet in excitement when they get a bite. Overhanging trees have to be cut back. Trout like the well-oxygenated water below minor waterfalls, so weirs have to be built and maintained and stone walls have to be mended, where ramblers knock them down, for the Dove flows through a popular part of the Peak National Park.

A man-sized job, you may think, for any water bailiff, but Dora is not only the lady she sounds; she is also in her mid-seventies. Her father was bailiff before her and she has been making perfection more perfect on his beat for the last thirty-odd years since he retired. I was lucky enough to spend some of the most glorious days of the summer of 1981 with her, making a film about her work and life which was shown as part of the 'In the Country' series.

She lives with Sampy, her border collie, in an isolated cottage owned by her employer, a Birmingham businessman, the third generation of whose family she has served. She waded in the water to catch the creepie-crawlies that trout regard as delicacies and she showed me the underwater caverns where the fish hide. I acted as her very unskilled labourer, helping to rebuild a weir and marvelled at her tact and patience dealing with trippers, whose idea of fun was to pull rocks out of the stone wall and heave them at her beloved fish.

She has had a hard but most rewarding life and she has the satisfaction of knowing that a lifetime of her loving care has added to the beauty of 'her' river and the welfare of 'her' fish.

61. Never Too Old To Be A Guinea Pig Fan

Friends are often surprised to see that I keep guinea pigs. They think they are pets that we should grow out of by the time we put on our first pair of long trousers. The odd thing is that, although I kept rabbits and white mice – and even tame rats and ferrets (though not at the same time!) – I never kept a guinea pig until I was well into my sixties.

Outside my study window is a wire-netted paddock of about half an acre where I rear a few pheasants and chickens that I hatch from eggs under broody hens. The hens repay the trouble by laying *real* free range eggs and the pheasants delight me as they strut around in front of the windows. The snag is that the turf has to be kept short so that the birds do not become wet and bedraggled in the sort of summers we normally have. The little paddock where they are reared is wedge-shaped and awkward to mow so that I began to doubt whether the reward was worth the trouble.

An advertisement offered a guinea pig to a good home for nothing because the owner was moving to a flat and, before we knew what hit us, Snowy had arrived. She was wonderfully tame and obviously had been shamelessly spoilt. She was also *very* pregnant! I hate seeing animals in cages and small hutches, so I gave her the freedom of the chicken paddock and the outhouses where I rear the young chicks. Quite soon, there were five miniature Snowies, about as big as your thumb, but fully furred, with open eyes – and enormous appetites.

Apart from scoffing the flaked maize and other goodies I put in their feeding trough, they grazed the grass in their paddock from dawn to dusk. It was absolutely astonishing how much they could consume – and even more incredible how fast they bred! Within months, there was a herd of multi-coloured animated grass-cutters, ranging from the pristine white of the matriarch Snowy, to black and piebald, and ginger of the boar I swapped with a fellow guinea pigman to introduce a dash of fresh blood.

Guinea pigs are favourite pets for children because they are soft and friendly; they don't bite when you pick them up and they are a convenient size for children to handle. I had always imagined that it must have taken countless generations to domesticate them from the wild and make them so naturally fearless.

The days of having to sweat it out with a lawn mower that needed petrol instead of flaked maize are long since gone! Indeed, they have mown their paddock so efficiently that there isn't enough grass left for them, so I have opened the gate and they have the freedom of the unfenced paddock by the house and can even get into the wood.

It has been fascinating to watch them gradually reverting to the habits of their wild ancestors. They dash for cover at any strange sound or sudden movement and they forage selectively for favourite diets. They have bitten out every leaf of clover for 20 or 30 yards from the entrance of their pen.

Although I do not shut them up at night, they retreat to their sleeping quarters at dusk, safe from foxes and owls, but they seem to have no defence against rats which plunder their young (until I trap them) so perhaps rats are not common where guinea pigs are native? Their peculiar whistle carries an incredible distance and calls their fellows to any new source of food as well as acting as a danger signal.

Occasionally one takes completely to the wild and chooses his own habitat among the dense tussocks in the wood, where he usually survives for a few weeks before disappearing, presumably falling victim to a prowling fox.

Nature is cruel like that but, if I were a guinea pig, I think I would prefer freedom with risks, to confinement in a stuffy hutch!

62. Nightmare Shape Of Fields To Come

My job recently took me to Northumberland for a few glorious days. I had always heard what a marvellously unspoilt wild county it was, so I expected vast wastes of craggy hills that would support nothing but a handful of wild sheep, sharing the inhospitable heather with even wilder grouse. Such wilderness is not much to my liking and I often shock artistic friends because the rugged grandeur of the Scottish Highlands or mountain tops of Wales do little for me. I prefer richer country – well-treed and able to grow grand cattle – to solitudes dotted with kilted natives shooting grouse or stalking deer.

So I was astonished to find that the land above Newcastle-on-Tyne was superb agricultural land with herds of beef cattle all set to restore our national reputation of serving the best roast beef in the world. The stock farms apparently grew their own feed, thus avoiding being rooked by the corn merchants. There were huge fields with gaudy pheasants picking an easy living (while it lasts) on prairies of golden stubble.

But I also saw a new phenomenon. Farming up there is obviously so prosperous that the latest equipment littered the fields and the modern fashion is to gather straw in circular bales. In purely corn-growing areas, straw is an embarrassment. The saddest sight of harvest is to see whole fields of straw laid waste by fire, leaving deserts of scorched earth, but in mixed farming country, the straw is used as bedding through the winter and spread over the land as rich manure in spring.

Until recently, the straw has been compressed in rectangular bales, 20 lbs or so dry weight, which are easy to stack neatly in ricks. But machines have a habit of growing bigger and bigger and the straw is now gathered in huge round bales, each weighing up to half a ton. They are far too large to move by hand and are moved with a type of fork-lift truck or fore-end loader on the tractor. They are so large that it would not be practical to stack them one on top of the other. The obvious thing is to line them up in rows along the edge of the fields and collect them, one by one, as they are required.

My first impression, on seeing platoons of them lined up along hedge bottoms, was that they would make the perfect windbreaks to shelter cattle and sheep from the belly-searching east winds that whip across the North Sea. Then I noticed that the land was so fertile that all the straw which had been harvested last year had not yet been needed or used. Rows of huge cylindrical bales had grass growing in their bottoms and, where they were close to hedges, the hedges were dying back.

There seems a danger that the rich pattern of hedgerowed fields that makes the landscape there so lovely is in danger of destruction, not by farmers grubbing out hedges, but as yet another penalty of allowing giant machines to master men. Taken to absurdity, a nightmare future landscape might be ruled into impersonal geometric squares, rhom-

A pile of massive circular bales

boids and rectangles by rows of soggy straw as ugly as concrete barriers to repel an invasion. I hope that the farmers there tumble to the danger before their hedges die.

Further inland, there are wild and desolate fells, but there are rich estates as well. It is small wonder that there seems to be almost a castle to the mile to defend them from the uncivilised savages who spent the Middle Ages organising raids from over the border to pillage the cattle and rape the women. The scale of Hadrian's Wall, constructed by puny manpower, centuries before bulldozers were dreamed about, boggles the imagination. The fortifications ran for backaching mile after mile and, admiring the feat against the setting sun, it was impossible not to compare it with modern 'achievements'.

Straw bales that threaten hedges, and combine harvesters so ungainly that they need 100-acre fields to cavort about in, put the achievements of modern man into humbling perspective.

63. My Roof Takes A Hammering

We have got a yaffle on our rooftop. The first we knew about it was when we heard what appeared to be someone hammering on the front door just as it was getting light in the morning. When I stuck my drowsy head out of the window above the porch, I was not that surprised to find nobody there. The dogs would have been barking their heads off if there had been. The hammering continued and I eventually located it over our own bedroom window.

The roof of the cottage is made of wooden shingles instead of conventional slates or tiles, so that it acts as an efficient sounding board. I still couldn't see what was kicking up such a din so, pulling on a shirt and trousers, I went out into the garden to have a look.

Perched below the apex, hammering the wooden shingles with all the enthusiasm of a blacksmith forging horseshoes, was the most beautiful green woodpecker I have ever seen. Or that was my first impression.

Countryfolk call green woodpeckers yaffles because of the noise they make. It echoes through lonely woods as peel after peel of satanic laughter. The view I got of the yaffle, hammering on my shingles, filled my eyes with pleasure. But it soon dawned on me that I had nothing to laugh about. What I had been watching – and listening to – was the systematic demolition of my own roof. The wretched bird had been hammering holes in it to get at the flies that had gone into hibernation between the warm, wooden roof shingles!

It reminded me that when we came here in the 1960s, the local doctor told us that Miss Jackson, who had lived here all her life, had told him that the woodpeckers bored holes in the roof every winter. When it happened to someone else, it seemed quite a joke and we told our friends that we had bought a cottage that was 'so rural that the woodpeckers kept it free of flies by boring holes in the roof to winkle them out'. It made the place unique and we couldn't imagine why the agents who had sold it hadn't included it among the amenities.

The green woodpecker where he should be – off my roof!

When we came to modernise the place, replacing the earth closet with modern sanitation, and installing the telephone and electricity, our builder said the whole place needed reroofing. The wooden shingles had rotted – and resembled a colander – but the planners said we would spoil the appearance if we reroofed with tiles or slates. As a result, our roof is still made of wood and the crevices between the shingles form perfect refuges for hibernating flies.

For reasons beyond my knowledge, it has taken the woodpeckers nearly twenty years to discover that our renovated cottage is still a banqueting hall far superior to the rotting tree stumps in the wood, where common woodpeckers feed. Fortunately yaffles are very shy birds because, though I would wish it no harm, I shall have to deter it from hammering holes in my roof.

But I shall not have to shoot it (which would be illegal anyway) or do anything drastic. All that I need do is to parade on the lawn at

197

daybreak, which will be quite enough to scare it off. This will be no hardship in winter because I am normally ready for my breakfast before it is light. In spring, when days lengthen, the flies will awaken from hibernation and leave the roof to feed and breed. Being a sensible chap, the yaffle will not waste his energy digging holes through the shingles in search of flies which have fled.

I am luckier than I thought.

64. Breakfast Date In Derbyshire

One of the programmes in the recent 'In the Country' series was recorded at Chatsworth in the golden days of September 1981. The Duke and Duchess of Devonshire were the hosts, and Angela Rippon, Joe Henson and I were guests. The head keeper, chief forester, and head gardener of the Chatsworth estate were there too, and the atmosphere was so relaxed and friendly that it proved the old adage that the only snobs are those who have nothing to be snobbish about.

At Chatsworth, with the Duke and Duchess of Devonshire, Angela Rippon and Joe Henson

So it is in other fields. Television is a highly competitive medium, but it is only those who don't quite make the grade who chuck their weight about vainly trying to convince the rest that they are star material. The folk who really reach the top are always the nicest to work with. Over the last three years, I have done a lot of programmes with Angela Rippon and I never worked with anyone I liked and respected more. Every programme I did taught me a few more refinements of my trade.

To get as far as she has, takes guts as well as flair. On one occasion, we had worked from 9 to 5 in the studio at Bristol, although she had got a cold that would have sent most people croaking for a sick note. The moment we finished, she jumped in her car and motored off to London to ride a horse in the show ring at Olympia. She works seven days a week and clocks up to 70,000 miles a year in her car, so it is natural that she doesn't suffer fools and layabouts gladly.

A London publisher wanted a photograph of her with me and my dog Tick, for the dust cover of a book we had both had a hand in. So we arranged to meet at her house near Tavistock early one Monday morning. The art director and photographer, who had spent the previous day prospecting for a suitable location, announced that we were going twenty miles to some crags in the wilds of Dartmoor. Angela suggested other equally photogenic craggy rocks above the river at the bottom of her garden, mentioning in passing that it was probably foggy on the moor.

The photographers thought they knew better, so off we trekked, only to find that it *was* foggy on the moor, far too foggy for photography! By the time we had returned to the rocks that she had originally suggested, it was pelting with rain so our picture on the dust cover is like looking through a mist darkly. Angela was far too professional to say 'I told you so' but it wasn't necessary to be a psychologist to read the meaning in her smile.

Neither the triumphs nor the trials of being in the public eye have had the slightest effect on her husband Chris, nor on her. He is as tough as they come: ex-Merchant Navy amateur boxer and successful business-man, with a big enough sense of humour to steamroller the pressures and share in the pleasures. When they come to stay with my wife and me, we always enjoy their visit.

When Angela introduced her first 'In the Country' programme three years ago, we started her first series by wandering round our wood with the dogs meeting the deer and the pheasants. The last number of the last series wound up with another visit to our wood where Honey, my white deer, obliged by bringing the wild deer up to feed, under floodlights, by the sitting-room window and to join with the family in wishing Angela the best of luck when she starts her breakfast television programmes.

65.   What Price Firewood?

The bureaucrats are blowing their tops because people are being over-charged for logs for the wood-burning stoves that are now the rage.

I can remember the days when you could have a ton of coal delivered for twenty-five bob – £1.25 in the washers we now use for currency. The coal didn't come in sacks. It came, with a horse and cart, to be tipped in the road outside the house and the customer was expected to get it into his coalshed with a wheel barrow. But still twenty-five bob! Petrol between the wars was about 1s 4d a gallon and you could buy the cheaper grades for 11d which I make equivalent to less than 5p. Now it is £1.60, or one pound twelve shillings in proper money, and heating oil has risen in proportion.

So it's no wonder that people have converted to wood-burning stoves because firewood was always a cheap fuel. But it isn't any more. You can't beat the law of supply-and-demand so that, as wood-burning stoves have risen in popularity, the demand for logs has increased – and so has the price.

When the fashion started a few years ago, there were thousands and thousands of elm trees, victims of the Dutch elm disease. Elm is a very tough wood, marvellous for its resistance to water, but very sullen as fuel on the fire. What is more, the grain blunders unpredictably as a drunkard so that it is not easy to split into neat logs. A great many people who had a few elms in their gardens had neither a chain saw with which to cut the dead ones down nor the skill to use it if they could have afforded one. So lots of spivs joined in competition with honest contractors to provide a 'service' in felling dead or dangerous elms. They charged so much for felling the trees that the price they got for the logs was a minor consideration.

Wood was cheap, so there was a boom in wood-burning stoves. The bonanza didn't last long. The initial supplies of easy wood soon went up chimneys in smoke, but folk who had installed the expensive stoves couldn't afford to scrap them. Demand for wood soon exceeded the supply – so the price went up. The spivs, who had made a packet felling trees, began to compete with each other to offer the highest price for standing timber.

Complaints from aggrieved customers soon uncovered rackets where the weight of timber purchased bore little resemblance to the amount delivered. One poor man was even charged with the *total* weight of lorry and load instead of simply the logs on the lorry!

I am not so worried about the mugs being fleeced as I am about the danger of felling whole woods that should have been left to mature into top class timber. This time last year, there was a lovely wood across the valley from our wood. Now the wood has gone, the roots have been cleared and the land ploughed. Our native hard woods, oak and ash and beech and sycamore, have taken a terrible hiding during the two world wars. Much of the land has been replanted with foreign firs which shade out all other plants and support practically no native wildlife. Other huge areas have been converted to agriculture, adding to the mountains of surplus food in the Common Market. It is easy enough to fell in minutes a tree which will take more than a human generation to grow a replacement.

The best thing for the future of our woodlands would be for logs to price themselves out of the market.

But perhaps there is a ray of hope. Mechanised farming has turned straw into an uneconomic crop except where huge numbers of cattle are kept. When the corn is harvested, the stubble is burned because it doesn't pay to harvest it. Some stove-makers are now selling stoves that will burn straw bales, and one farmer friend of mine now heats his house for nothing but the labour cost of harvesting his straw. If the price of logs increases enough, perhaps we shall see the day when straw is a viable fuel and there will be no more scorched earth at harvest time.

66. Drop Your Sights In Bad Weather

I believe that there is room in the countryside for all sorts of conflicting interests, but the opposition to the ban on shooting duck in the hard weather we have been suffering makes me sick. Wild duck are cunning birds which are normally capable of outwitting sportsmen pursuing them. In order to succeed, the sportsmen have to go out at dusk and dawn and endure the rigours of windswept mudflats and estuaries. Often they have to go to the length of digging a trench in the mud and

Inland wildfowling on flooded marshland

shivering in concealment there until the wildfowl fly into gunshot.

Not being a good shot, the sport doesn't attract me because, if I am going to make a fool of myself, I prefer to do so in comfort. But I do remember going out on to the flat saltings of the Wash with old Kensie Thorpe, the professional wildfowler, who imitated the calls of wild geese and curlew with such success that they actually flew down and allowed us to film them.*

It would, of course, have been just as easy to use a gun as a camera. The weary birds never even suspected that predatory men were almost within spitting distance. To outwit them to such an extent demanded the skill of a primitive hunting man and I can understand the thrill of modern sportsmen who can exercise similar skills, though 'capturing' them on film was all the thrill I wanted.

But the sort of weather we have been having this winter tips the odds in the sportsmen's favour until it becomes butchery more than the age-old contest between hunter and hunted. Hunger tames the wildest beast because the will to live overcomes the natural caution. Instinct says that if you don't eat, you die. Any other peril is a lesser risk. So, in very hard weather, the shyest ducks and geese and waders grow careless in running water where they would not normally venture. It is often easy to creep up on them because long spells without food slow them up physically as well as mentally.

Those that feed on the tideline can only feed when the water is at the right depth and daylight fills their needs. If tides and sunrise happen to combine to give the worst conditions, it limits the possibility of getting their fill. Add to their difficulties the perils of wildfowlers with guns, determined to exploit the opportunity of big and easy bags, and the birds are really up against it.

So there is now a law that prohibits the shooting of wildfowl in long spells of continuous hard weather. Duck shooters say that they are responsible people and know enough about their quarry to treat it with respect and avoid harrying it in very bad conditions. They resent the implication that it is necessary to pass a law protecting the birds they say they wouldn't shoot.

This may well be so for the majority, but there is no shadow of doubt

* *see One Man and His Dog*

that a lot of duck and geese are shot in such appalling conditions that protection is vital for their survival. If it is true that the culprits are only a handful of irresponsible 'cowboys', the responsible chaps, who say they wouldn't offend anyhow, have nothing to lose and I fail to see why they complain. By doing so, they bring themselves into disrepute, handing ammunition to their opposition.

I am delighted therefore that the Royal Society for the Protection of Birds and other pressure groups have persuaded Parliament to ban the shooting of species that are particularly vulnerable during protracted periods of bad weather.

But I think the ban should have gone further. In times like this, rarities get blown in to our shores by storm or flee from even worse weather on the continent. Then the bird watchers – the 'Twitchers' – converge on them to add them to their little lists. The poor birds have no means of knowing whether they are carrying guns or cameras or notebooks, so they are driven from feeding as surely as if the eccentric 'Twitchers' had murder in their hearts.

The law against shooting in severe weather should include disturbance of any avoidable kind.

67. Showing Me The Way To Go Home

If I ever owned a bump of locality, it was hammered out of shape at birth. I reckon to know my own wood like the back of my hand, as I should do because I spend at least an hour or so there every day I am not working away from home. Yet if I am out there after dark on a moonless night or in a thick fog, I sometimes have no more idea of the direction of the house than if I were dropped in the middle of a desert. I have to keep walking until I stumble across the boundary fence and then follow the fence until I arrive in the yard at the back of the house.

It's just the same when I'm driving in a strange town. A couple of circuits of the one-way system that seems to plague all towns and I have no more idea where to set my course than from the middle of Hampton Court maze. I envy the chaps in the Bible who went round Jericho seven times until the walls fell down.

Uneducated animals and birds put us to shame. Swallows come all the way from Africa, starlings and wood pigeons navigate from Scandinavia and racing pigeons have always amazed me.

Nobody knows how they do it. A popular theory suggested that racing pigeons navigate by the stars. To back up the theory, some pigeons were put in a building: there were no windows, but the ceiling was domed, like the sky, with lights at the spots where the stars would have shone – if the sky had been visible. The pigeons showed signs of trying to escape in the right direction, despite the fact that no external landmarks were visible. The ceiling was then rotated so that the stars appeared to shine from the wrong direction and, so it is said, the birds were deceived into trying to escape where the phoney stars directed.

I have never been very convinced by this, as pigeon races are flown in daylight and I can't see that it is likely they would navigate by stars.

Another theory was that migratory birds – and presumably racing pigeons – have some sort of magnet in their heads that acts as a conventional compass. This seemed equally unlikely, but there is

The miracle navigator – the swallow

recent evidence to suggest that there is some substance in the idea. Some scientists claim to have isolated material that reacts to magnetic forces, not only of migratory birds, but ordinary animals as well, from the bone of skulls.

This fired my interest because I often come across stories of dogs and cats that found their way home over long distances when lost on holiday or sold to new owners. One cunning rural rascal claimed to have sold the same dog five or six times – he always escaped and came home in the misguided confidence that his mercenary owner would not banish him to strangers again.

But the most remarkable case I know, at first hand, was of a white foxhound that belonged to a Shropshire man who made a living catching foxes for their skins. He took a few working terriers and some

208

foxhounds, retired from hunting, to an island off the west coast of Scotland where foxes were particularly common. Within a day or so, his white hound went missing. He looked everywhere for her, but there was no sign and he came to the conclusion that she must have fallen to her death over the cliffs.

He decided to go home, and asked the ferryman to catch her if she turned up, promising a reward for her return. Nothing was heard for six months. Then the hound arrived at the door of his Shropshire cottage, thin as a skeleton and blind in one eye.

When she first realised she was lost, she must have got across to the mainland before her owner missed her, as the ferryman never saw a sign of her. She then found her own way home, across 400 miles of strange country. She apparently lived off the land, catching her own food, because the cause of her blindness was that someone had shot her in the eye.

Her feat fills my mind with as much wonder as migratory birds or racing pigeons – and I am rather glad that even the cleverest scientists don't know how it is done. It cuts us human know-alls down to size!

68. All In The Stars When I'm Stuck In The Snow

My three pet hates are horoscopes, standing in queues and travelling by rail. I recently had a bellyful of all of them.

I was supposed to be in the television studio in Bristol by half past nine. So I set out at half past six. Being an habitually punctual chap, I always allow a bit for hard lines. The distance is 128 miles from door to door and I can normally drive it comfortably in just under two hours.

Most of the journey is by motorway, so if I didn't hang around too much I calculated there would be time for a leisurely breakfast in the canteen before I started work. Visions of fried bacon and sausage, black pudding and eggs with toast and marmalade washed down by coffee faded before I got to the main road. Not only was it snowing hard, making it necessary to go flat out at the drifts, but the man on the radio said it would get worse.

I sacrificed my ambitions of breakfast, parked my car at Lichfield Station and caught the 7.32. The man in the booking office said it would connect with the 8.15 from Birmingham which would get me to Bristol by a quarter past ten. He was a little over-optimistic. Such office-bound types usually are. It's one of the things I dislike about tains.

Although we were late in Birmingham and the Bristol train was also late, it didn't start late enough. It was just disappearing as I got on to the platform. This gave me time to telephone my wife and tell her that if the prophets of doom and gloom on the radio said there was a pile-up on the motorway, I shouldn't be in it. I should be on the train instead, and it was in the lap of the gods what time – if ever – I got back. I asked her to ring the chap I was working with and tell him that although I would be late, at least I was on the way and the amended time was 11.15.

But by that time, we were stuck a mile outside Cheltenham and we finally crept into Cheltenham Station at half past one. The trouble that kept stopping us for hours at a time appeared to be the ice that jammed the points. Some brilliant boffin had invented a cure which was a crib of

210

The author in a philosophical mood

a painter's blowlamp. It was fired by bottled gas and produced a very hot flame which, in theory, heated the points and melted the ice. This wonder of modern science probably worked like a charm in a draught-free drawing-office where the geniuses who invented it worked. What they had obviously forgotten was that there's usually a wind in a blizzard, and the flame that was supposed to heat the points kept blowing out, so that the points were never unfrozen.

There wasn't a restaurant car so by mid-afternoon we were getting more than peckish. Having expected breakfast in Bristol and swallowed nothing but my pride, I eventually reached the state of being ready to line up for a British Rail sandwich, which I dislike about as much as queuing and horoscopes. But hunger will tame even the wild animals in a circus and I am not particularly lion-hearted when my belly is compressed against my backbone.

We didn't reach Bristol until half past five in the afternoon and there were no trains back that night. So I had plenty of time to read. Sadly, I had nothing more interesting than the *Daily Express* which I had read from cover to cover by the time we got held up on the line outside Cheltenham. So acute was my boredom that I even read my horoscope, which said as follows: 'Taurus, April 21 – May 20. Take things philosophically. Whittle down the day's activities to essentials, and keep timetables very flexible, as it will be impossible to gauge how long it will take you to get through what has to be done.'

How right it was! I still feel the same about queuing and railways – but I shall have a sneaky peep at my horoscope again. It might tip me off when to fill in the pools coupon!

Index